THE CHALLENGE OF
LIBRARY MANAGEMENT

ALA Editions purchases fund advocacy, awareness, and accreditation programs for library professionals worldwide.

THE CHALLENGE OF
LIBRARY MANAGEMENT

Leading with Emotional Engagement

Wyoma vanDuinkerken & Pixey Anne Mosley

AMERICAN LIBRARY ASSOCIATION | CHICAGO 2011

Wyoma vanDuinkerken is the coordinator of cataloging record support and an associate professor at Texas A&M University Libraries. She has also held roles at Texas A&M as the interim head of cataloging staff, coordinator of monographs acquisitions, reference librarian for Islamic studies, and project leader for the implementation of virtual reference. Prior to her arrival in Texas, she managed documentation and support and customer service response for a library software company in Canada and worked with the Office of Strategic Business Initiatives of the University of Illinois, Urbana-Champaign, managing an extensive project portfolio.

Pixey Anne Mosley is the head of collection support services and a professor at Texas A&M University Libraries and has recently served as the interim director of the university's academic integrity office. She has published extensively on management in libraries with articles in *Library Leadership & Management* and *Reference & User Services Quarterly* and has authored two previous books, *Staying Successful as a Middle Manager* and *Transitioning from Librarian to Middle Manager*. She is currently the co-associate editor for *Library Leadership & Management,* the official journal of the Library Leadership and Management Association. She previously served as the coordinator of instructional services and head of access services at Texas A&M and as the information technology librarian at the University of North Texas. Prior to her career in librarianship, she was an aerospace engineer in the corporate sector, working for Boeing and Allied-Signal.

Printed in the United States of America

15 14 13 12 11   5 4 3 2 1

While extensive effort has gone into ensuring the reliability of the information in this book, the publisher makes no warranty, express or implied, with respect to the material contained herein.

ISBNs: 978-0-8389-1102-0 (paper); 978-0-8389-9280-7 (PDF); 978-0-8389-9281-4 (ePub); 978-0-8389-9282-1 (Mobipocket); 978-0-8389-9283-8 (Kindle). *For more information on digital formats, visit the ALA Store at alastore.ala.org and select eEditions.*

Library of Congress Cataloging-in-Publication Data
VanDuinkerken, Wyoma.
  The challenge of library management : leading with emotional engagement / Wyoma vanDuinkerken and Pixey Anne Mosley.
      p. cm.
  Includes bibliographical references and index.
  ISBN 978-0-8389-1102-0 (alk. paper)
  1. Library administration. 2. Organizational change--Management. 3. Leadership. 4. Library administration--Problems, exercises, etc. I. Mosley, Pixey Anne. II. Title.
  Z678.V36 2011
  025.1--dc22

                                                                    2011011349

Book design in Liberation Serif and Melbourne by Casey Bayer.
Cover illustration © Maugli/Shutterstock, Inc.

⊚ This paper meets the requirements of ANSI/NISO Z39.48–1992 (Permanence of Paper).

CONTENTS

PREFACE

CONTINUOUS CHANGE IN libraries: one sees it emphasized time after time in conference programs and in the scholarly and popular literature of librarianship. Changes in service delivery models, organizational structure and staffing, workflows and processes, and facilities are happening across the entire world of libraries. But have you ever thought about why some changes are more successful than others? Or asked why some organizations seem more resilient when faced with continuous change while others seem to struggle with every new change endeavor? This book offers some possible answers to these questions as it looks at the softer skills of change leadership in the context of the literature from the business and social science disciplines. How a change is communicated and the manner in which employees are engaged or isolated from the decision-making process during the planning and implementation stages of a change can play a key role in the future long-term success of the change.

The chapters of this book are arranged around several themes, and each chapter ends with some exercises that a reader can use as a reflective or discussion tool in thinking about leading change effectively. Chapters 1 through 3 help readers understand some of the psychological, sociological, and organizational culture aspects of the change experience in libraries. These chapters also give insights into the particular skills needed to be an effective change leader and why some highly effective managers or team leaders can run into difficulties when faced with leading a major change initiative. Chapters 4 and 5 lay out the chronology of initiating, planning, and implementing a change. In evaluating failed change initiatives, one common problem comes from having skipped a key phase of the planning or implementation process in trying to meet an overly optimistic deadline. These chapters emphasize that truly successful change initiatives cannot be rushed as a leader is developing individual buy-in and building an organizational culture that will sustain the change. Chapters 6 and 7 address specific challenges that can undermine or reinforce participation in the change, and its ultimate success. These chapters also give tips and advice on how one effectively addresses unanticipated delays or conflicts that can arise during any major change initiative. Often change leaders need effective crisis management leadership skills when dealing with disruptions to the planning and implementation process. Chapter 8 explains how one can objectively assess one's own performance as a change leader and evaluate the overall success of the change for lessons learned in leading a subsequent change in the future. Finally, chapter 9 discusses the specific issues one can face for different types of changes, such as organizational structure, construction/renovation changes, and personnel/workflow changes. The chapter also presents information on the impact of major changes to help one understand what the culture can adjust to more easily, ongoing medium-level changes or huge "turn everything on its head" changes.

The material for this book is gathered from literature across the disciplines of management, human resources, psychology, organizational theory, and librarianship and the authors' own experiences from having been leaders, participants, or observers in many change initiatives in different fields and institutions. Any examples are fictional in nature and are developed as composites based on trends seen in libraries across the country. Ironically, during the course of writing this book, the authors themselves were swept up in major organizational changes, with Wyoma moving from her coordinator role in acquisitions to a similar management and change leader role for catalog record support, and Pixey changing managerial responsibilities from access services to cataloging and shelving operations and serving in a university-level administrative role during a budgetary realignment. Along with this, they went through several changes in organizational visioning and renovations of the public spaces and collection stacks.

Finally, the authors would like to thank those individuals who provided us with encouragement and support during the course of writing this book and without whom this book would probably not have been completed. This includes Wyoma's husband, Desmond Ng, and children Gabriel and Logan, and Pixey's husband, Joel Kitchens. We would also like to thank our friend and colleague Wendi Kaspar for her support in helping us to keep things in perspective and stay focused on what was professionally important. Finally, a thanks to our ALA editor, Chris Rhodes, for his support and flexibility in getting contract details ironed out, providing feedback on chapter drafts, and extending deadlines while we settled into our new jobs.

CHAPTER ONE

CHANGE IN LIBRARIES

Common sense is not so common.

—Voltaire

ALTHOUGH THE QUOTE above is almost 250 years old, Voltaire's statement seems particularly true in today's constantly changing library environment. Common sense is based on a collective consciousness of shared ideas, knowledge, and understanding. However, when change occurs, the knowledge underpinning that common sense is altered and it seems that common sense gets thrown out the window. Leaders feel their decisions are based on obvious common sense, so of course everyone should embrace those decisions enthusiastically. Secure in this knowledge, they marginalize apparent resistance and are perpetually surprised when a planned change stalls or even fails. Similarly, when changes are thrust upon individuals and stress over job security blinds them, it is difficult for them to plug into that shared understanding and find the commonsense grounding for having confidence in their work and positive engagement with others.

National estimates indicate that one third of all workers in the United States report that their jobs are "often" or "always" stressful.[1] Today's fast-paced, ever-changing lifestyle is taking a toll on employees, and as a result common sense is being replaced by work-related stress reactions. Although there are common and predictable stressors related to change, how a person reacts to those stressors can differ. Given a high degree of uncertainty over organizational change, employees and managers can feel anxiety and confusion about the unknown and as a consequence utilize basic defenses such as distrust in leadership, withdrawal from the organization, and self-protection, causing even positive changes to stumble and falter. Change, however, is a natural part of life and of contemporary organizations if they hope to be successful in the future. In libraries, the greatest challenge we face in this new technological era is the recognition that our past strengths will become our liabilities if we do not change to meet the needs of the changing society.[2]

DEFINING HOW LIBRARIES ARE DIFFERENT

Libraries, like all organizations, are facing a period of rapid technological growth that is changing societies around the world. Patrons are developing higher expectations of library services and often end up using these services differently than the way they were used in the past. Though it was ten years ago as the opening speaker at the 2000 American Library Association's Second Congress on Professional Education, Wendy Schultz was particularly visionary as she pointed to a number of societal issues that are affecting our profession.[3] The items she noted are even more valid today and are impacting all types of libraries at significant levels:

- the acceleration of the pace of change
- the ubiquity of technological innovation
- rapid globalization
- economic issues
- expanding educational formats and opportunities
- demographic shifts
- population diversity
- changing workplace structures and ethics
- altered worker demands
- changes in customer expectations and lifestyles

As a result of these factors, libraries and librarians need to redefine collections and services to keep up with the changing environment in order to meet the needs of their customers and remain relevant. However, according to Stephens and Russell, although librarians are aware of these issues that impact our profession, it does not necessarily mean librarians understand the issues and, more important, whether they believe that knowledge of these issues is used by management when they are planning and implementing change in library organizations.[4] It is because of this misunderstanding that resistance to change occurs.

In addition, it is important for managers to remember that they view change differently than employees. According to Strebel, both managers and employees recognize that vision and leadership promote successful change, but not all managers recognize the ways in which employees commit to the advancement of successful change.[5] Strebel believes that top-level administrators see "change as an opportunity to strengthen the business by aligning operations with strategy, to take on new professional challenges and risks, and to advance their careers. For many employees, however, including middle managers, change is neither sought after nor welcomed. It is disruptive and intrusive. It upsets the balance."[6]

While there is a plethora of change-management literature available from the business and human development fields, it can still be challenging to understand how to apply it in the library environment.[7] Libraries are not commercial retailers, though they do share some customer service objectives. Though they do have to worry about their budgets and look to the future, libraries are not private corporations, with profit as a bottom line and layoffs or downsizing of active employees as the regularly used tool to manage budgets or implement change initiatives. Similarly, few libraries are stand-alone nonprofit organizations, though they share some "public good" characteristics with this sector. Separate from the small business sector, libraries are usually part of a larger educational or civic-based entity that will have a well-developed employee culture with established rules, policies, and procedures. According to Kreitz, adding to the problem are demographic changes in the workforce today, along with the increasing international competition caused by globalization of markets; these have increased the amount of diversity organizations must manage, both within the organization and outside of it.[8] Many argue that leaders who are interested in surviving and thriving in the world today must use their diverse workplace to their advantage, and in order to do this successfully, managers must redefine how they lead.[9] Because of this hybrid identity, successfully introducing change in this culture can introduce particular challenges. It takes a particular type of hybrid leader to successfully implement and manage ongoing organizational change in a library environment.

According to Stephens and Russell, there is very little research on organizational change in libraries and the necessary leadership characteristics needed to accomplish change.[10] Instead, the majority of literature on this topic is based largely on corporate enterprises, not libraries. This book will offer insights into developing the skills to be an effective change leader in libraries, both in the context of traditional leadership models still supported by many administrations and with the next generation of employees who expect a different workplace culture in terms of support and engagement than previous generations.

Although libraries are different, library managers and administrators know libraries and understand the culture, so one has to ask why it is still difficult for them to lead change effectively. There are several contributing factors. The key is that libraries have a wider degree of cultural variation across the organization than one will find in the business world.[11] Generally, competitive companies mimic each other's style of operation in finding the most profitable management practices and establishing an employee and organizational culture. A lot of financial and personnel resources go into creating groupthink programs and mandating the desired employee culture and conduct. Corporate culture influences the manner in which employees act and work together and strongly impact how things get completed.[12] Perhaps from having professional roots in the concepts of free speech, freedom of information, and academic institutions where inquiry is encouraged, libraries have not pursued this management model with the fervor of the corporate world. A library's organizational culture with its task and operational departments, specialized professional staffing models, and generally stable employee base can have a significant impact on the success of change initiatives. Understanding organizational culture is discussed in more detail in chapter 3.

While an administrator may establish priorities or set a general tone, there is usually a higher degree of employee freedom and less actual retaliation for speaking up or questioning authority. While open disapproval of an idea and a moderate degree of active or passive resistance may result in one being given less leadership responsibilities or even marginal evaluations, it seldom will actually result in the termination of an employee. This is unlike the corporate environment, where often standing out from the group makes one a target for the first round of any staff reduction activities. The difference in libraries is particularly pronounced in academic institutions, where librarians have some manner of faculty status that provides academic freedom protection to express their opinions.[13] This means that managerial engagement on the change becomes even more critical for overall success, but can still be extremely difficult for a manager to accomplish.

MANAGERIAL CHALLENGES

The first obvious challenge is that a manager may know one library or department, but what about when she is asked to lead change somewhere else? This could be as a formal transfer or newly hired manager or as a crossdepartmental team leader brought in for an "outsider" perspective. The new department or team may have a different organizational culture than the one the leader previously worked in.[14] This "outsider perspective" can exist to encourage library staff to exchange new ideas and to try new workflow processes in order to create an efficient work environment. By creating this learning environment libraries will be able to meet the expectations of students, faculty, and staff.[15] This is discussed in more detail in chapter 7.

Most contemporary library departments are a mixture of different types of people. However, even within this mix, there will tend to be an organizational subculture based on the library's role or environment. An office with open architecture and a lot of teamwork or interaction in supporting a service, such as making sure a service desk is sufficiently staffed on the fly, will have a different culture than an office where most of the work is accomplished by individuals with explicitly defined tasks and less reason to develop a sense of inter-reliance. However, even if the basic functional support is the same, one cannot assume that a department subculture is the same at different institutions. Suppose in one library, a reference desk is staffed based on a rigid, mediated scheduling process with predefined backups to call if someone has a conflict or gets sick. The subculture in this reference department will be very different from one where a basic schedule is set up but individuals are expected to round up their own replacement coverage when they need to be out. In the latter environment, teamwork becomes a more critical cultural element, and individuals will be more likely to speak or act out publicly against someone whom they feel is not pulling their weight by always getting substitutes. In the former, there may be grumbles at having to cover for someone a lot, but the expectation will be that the scheduler will handle any performance-related reporting. For a manager walking into a new dynamic as a change agent, there is a high potential for misinterpretation based on the cultural symbolism attributed to a comment.

It does not hurt to ask if the culture can be changed to take advantage of positives from other models. But it is critical to recognize the difference between what can be changed and what cannot or should not. While a certain degree of firmness in commitment to an initiative is expected of administrators and managers, it is the author's observation that academic institutions are less likely to adopt the ultimatum approach that can lead to formal litigation or bring in institutional scrutiny of human resources practices. Additionally, many academic institutions are based on a model of shared governance to some degree. This can vary from institution to institution but serves to reiterate the value of stakeholder buy-in for major changes. In this respect, libraries should follow the institutional trend. For example, if you are a manager or administrator who does not believe in or support tenure-track status for librarians, going to an institution that is based on this model will turn into an exercise in frustration when you have much less flexibility in reassigning senior librarians or have to accept that a full-time librarian does not equal forty hours of focused work due to the need for release time to conduct research or professional service. It is important to avoid trying to directly change situations that resemble the irresistible force and the immovable object. Chapters 3 and 6 delve more deeply into organizational culture impact on change initiatives.

Secondly, even though library managers have come up through the ranks, most have not had extensive formal training in change leadership. A basic management course might have been a part of the manager's MLS program some years ago, but management philosophies change, and it is sometimes more difficult to see this as one is immersed in the work environment. The library industry has always been focused on service to others, and as a result librarians often forget about service to themselves. We are passionate about developing our skills as librarians to support the needs of our users, but we've neglected developing ourselves as leaders.[16] Additionally, most librarian jobs, particularly in larger libraries, involve an expectation of one developing as a specialist with a narrow area of expertise. This is actually a deterrent to becoming a successful change leader, which requires one to become more of a generalist who looks at multiple ideas from a wide range of perspectives. Finally, depending on the organizational structure, the manager may or may not have access to effective mentoring and growth opportunities through a formal training program.[17] However, even with mentoring, workshops, and self-development, leading change can be one of the most difficult challenges a manager faces because it involves individual human beings who will react in an unpredictable manner when faced with specific changes. The authors have frequently heard peers describe leading in academia as a whole and libraries in particular as "attempting to herd cats."[18]

When the leadership activities involve significant change and introduce high levels of emotion into the situation, cats can quickly transform from independent but domesticated house cats into a group of wild mountain lions. This is because the same stresses associated with change trigger the classic fight-or-flight instincts.[19] To effectively lead change in this environment, leaders and managers must avoid responding to triggers that could lead to abuse of administrative power; they must understand what is motivating employees in their resistance, and actively work to counter it using positive engagement techniques that encourage the employee to come down from a highly emotional state and restore rational, thoughtful deliberation and empowerment to the process. According to Warnken, if change is to be successful, then the process to achieve this change needs to be well planned and communicated and it must be inclusive.[20] Unfortunately, this can be very difficult to accomplish for some managers, and they will often make predictable mistakes before learning to effectively lead change. In truth, some managers do not understand the role of emotions in employee motivation, find change leadership particularly challenging, and never reach an effective understanding of the emotional underpinnings that can make one change highly successful and another a dismal failure.

APPLYING BUSINESS MODELS

Earlier in this chapter, it was pointed out that libraries do not fit precisely into the business model in the products they provide and in their personnel policies. However, this does not mean that there are not tools that can be applied from the business sector in developing one's leadership identity and to help with managing change.[21] The human resource development and management literature offers a multitude of articles that analyze and provide insights into factors that are important to leading change. They include areas such as employee empowerment and motivation, facilitating communication, team building, involvement, rewards and recognition, and training and development. Even though a library may not be able to implement an entire management philosophy, such as Total Quality Management, *Good to Great*, Nordstrom's or Disney's customer service models, or Tom Peters's leadership models, there may be room to adopt and apply some component pieces.[22]

One important element is for managers to realize that there is no magic formula for leading change that will automatically apply to every situation or promise success every time. Because an individual's acceptance or resistance to a change is based on an emotional and personal response, this response can change depending on the individual's perceptions of the proposed change and the personal impact. An employee who is the best cheerleader for one change can become the resistance leader for another.

For example, suppose Mike's department has a vacancy occur because Peter left. After discussing the departmental needs with the administration, Mike redefines the position to new organizational needs and plans to distribute the critical components of what Peter had been doing, such as processing patron requests, among other staff. Marci hears that the department is not going to be able to replace Peter. Given that Marci did not have a high opinion of Peter's level of productivity, she does not think this is a big deal and actually supports getting someone in for the new duties no one has time to do now. As her colleagues are reacting emotionally about the lost position, Marci speaks up in support of the administrative decision to redefine the focus of the position's responsibilities. Mike breathes a sigh of relief at having some grassroots support. Fast-forward six weeks: Mike meets with Marci and abruptly begins to discuss the need for her to take on some of the patron requests responsibilities. Marci did not see this coming and does not take the news well. Mike is shocked at her resistance to being a team player in the reassigned responsibilities. From Marci's perspective, she was able to support the change earlier because it did not affect her personally. Now that she has learned it will impact her own workload, her emotional perspective has changed. Ultimately, because he did not anticipate that her response would differ from in the past, Mike has to now backtrack and rebuild buy-in at a personal level with Marci.

KEYS TO SUCCESS

In bringing together the introductory ideas about change in libraries, there are several points to keep in mind.

- Successful change does not happen in a vacuum or simply as a mandate, but requires the engagement of stakeholders at multiple levels.
- In looking at comparative models and management and leadership programs, it is important to consider what will and will not work for this particular library environment and organizational culture.
- Business models that can be adopted most effectively within libraries are those that focus on emotional leadership and communication-based engagement.
- Success in leading change requires that one adopt a broad perspective of situational and servant-based leadership that adapts to the different needs of different changes.[23]
- One must set aside one's ego and symbolic baggage in how an administrator, manager, or team leader should act and go the extra mile in being responsive to the needs of the individuals that are having change enacted upon them.

THINKING EXERCISES

1. What aspects of your library fit the various organizational models described in this chapter (corporate, commercial, nonprofit, civic, academic)?

2. How would you describe your organizational culture toward explaining decisions?

3. Does the organizational or administrative/managerial communication model satisfy or match the expectations for information from the
front lines? If not, where does it break down and what can you do to
improve it?

4. Think of three or four leaders who have had the biggest positive impact
on your professional or personal development. Write down what they did
that made them stand out (the characteristics you most admired or would
want to emulate). Now repeat the exercise for leaders who have had the
biggest negative impact on you. Examine the two lists for guidance in
traits to adopt and techniques to avoid as you continue to develop as a
leader. You can even make yourself a "reminder" pinup for those leadership traits and techniques that are most important or most difficult.

NOTES

1. Lawrence Murphy and Steven Sauter, "The USA Perspective: Current Issues and
   Trends in the Management of Work Stress," *Australian Psychologist* 38 (July 2003):
   151–57.
2. Patricia Battin, "Leadership in a Transformational Age," in *Mirage of Continuity:
   Reconfiguring Academic Information Resources for the 21st Century,* ed. Brian L.
   Hawkins and Patricia Battin (Washington, DC: Council on Library and Information
   Resources: Association of American Universities, 1998): 271–77.
3. American Library Association, "Second Congress on Professional Education,
   November 17–19, 2000, Final Report of the Steering Committee," www.ala.org/ala/
   educationcareers/education/2ndcongressonpro/2ndcongressprofessionaleducationfinal.
   cfm.
4. Denise Stephens and Keith Russell, "Organizational Development, Leadership,
   Change, and the Future of Libraries," *Library Trend* 53 (Summer 2004): 238–57.
5. Paul Strebel, "Why Do Employees Resist Change?" *Harvard Business Review* 74
   (May-June 1996): 86–92.
6. Ibid.
7. Yannick Fronda and Jean-Luc Moriceau, "I Am Not Your Hero: Change Management
   and Culture Shocks in a Public Sector Corporation," *Journal of Organizational
   Change Management* 21, no. 5 (2008): 589–609; Richard Cooney and Graham Sewell,
   "Shaping the Other: Maintaining Expert Managerial Status in a Complex Change
   Management Program," *Group and Organization Management* 33 (December 2008):
   685–711; Kannan Mohan, Peng Xu, and Balasubramaniam Ramesh, "Improving the
   Change-Management Process," *Communication of the ACM* 51 (May 2008): 59–64;
   Eric B. Dent and Susan Galloway Goldberg, "Challenging 'Resistance to Change,'"
   Journal of Applied Behavioral Science 35 (March 1999): 25–41.
8. Patricia A. Kreitz, "Best Practices for Managing Organizational Diversity," *Journal of
   Academic Librarianship* 34 (March 2008): 101–20.

9. Ibid.
10. Denise Stephens and Keith Russell, "Organizational Development."
11. Ibid, 246.
12. Samuel Olu Adeyoyin, "Managing the Library's Corporate Culture for Organizational Efficiency, Productivity, and Enhanced Service," *Library Philosophy and Practice* 3 (Spring 2006): 1–14.
13. Blaise Cronin, "Knowledge Management, Organizational Culture and Anglo-American Higher Education," *Journal of Information Science* 27, no. 3 (2001): 129–37.
14. Ibid.
15. Donald E. Riggs, "What's in Store for Academic Libraries? Leadership and Management Issues," *Journal of Academic Librarianship* 23 (January 1997): 3–7.
16. Donna Nicely and Beth Dempsey, "Building a Culture of Leadership: ULC's Executive Leadership Institute Fills Libraries' Biggest Training Void," *Public Libraries* 44 (2005): 297–300.
17. Gail Munde, "Beyond Mentoring: Toward the Rejuvenation of Academic Libraries," *Journal of Academic Librarianship* 26 (May 2000): 171–75.
18. Warren Bennis, *Managing People Is Like Herding Cats* (Provo, UT: Executive Excellence, 1997)
19. Aaron T. Beck, "Beyond Belief: A Theory of Modes, Personality, and Psychopathology," in *Frontiers of Cognitive Therapy,* ed. Paul M. Salkovskis (New York: Guilford, 1996), 1–25.
20. Paula Warnken, "The Impact of Technology on Information Literacy Education in Libraries," *Journal of Academic Librarianship* 30 (March 2004): 151–56.
21. Gisela M. von Dran and Jennifer Cargill, eds., *Catalysts for Change* (New York: Haworth, 1993).
22. Armand V. Feigenbaum, *Quality Control: Principles, Practice, and Administration* (McGraw-Hill, Collins, 2001); and Thomas Peters and Robert Waterman, *In Search of Excellence: Lessons from America's Best-Run Companies* (New York: Harper & Row, 1982).
23. Riggs, "What's in Store for Academic Libraries?"; Vicki Williamson, "Relationships and Engagement: The Challenges and Opportunities for Effective Leadership and Change Management in a Canadian Research Library," *Library Management* 29, nos. 1/2 (2008): 29–40; H. Frank Cervone, "Working through Resistance to Change by Using the Competing Commitments Model," *International Digital Library Perspectives* 23, no. 3 (2007): 250–53; Kurt Lewin, "Action Research and Minority Problems," *Journal of Social Issues* 2 (1946): 34–46.

CHAPTER TWO

THE HUMAN FACTOR

Without changing our pattern of thought, we will not be able to solve the problems we created with our current patterns of thought.

—Albert Einstein

WHEN DEALING WITH organizational changes, the most common reason for an initiative to flounder, encounter delays, or even fail is that the manager or leader has not taken into consideration the human factor. According to Gotsill and Natchez, managers who acknowledge an employee's natural tendency to fight change take the critical first step toward a positive change outcome.[1] This factor recognizes that the instruments of change are actually individuals with very personal, emotion-based reactions to change.[2] Pragmatic leaders who ignore the power of the emotional response of the stakeholders or apply the philosophy that "they will just need to get over it" will never be as successful as change leaders who recognize the power of emotion in motivation or de-motivation of an employee in supporting a change.[3] Before readers cringe at the idea that this chapter is all about being touchy-feely and requires managers to become professional psychologists who must help every staff member work through emotional quagmires, let us say that this is *not* what we are proposing. Rather, by gaining an understanding of the underlying emotions associated with change, managers can become more effective at planning, announcing, and carrying through changes and respond more positively and constructively to behaviors manifested out of change-related emotions.

The same way a senior professor in electrical engineering who is doing groundbreaking telecommunications research can have difficulty communicating about the components of basic circuitry to an undergraduate student, administrators who have immersed themselves in detecting and planning for the future of the library can have difficulty communicating the context of their vision to the front-line staff member, whose world revolves around an isolated task such as processing interlibrary loan requests or retrieving on-hold books. Similarly, most individuals who have chosen to pursue leadership or management roles in any profession have a more robust natural response to change. According to Drucker, a change leader sees change as an opportunity and will have a more resilient perspective on the disruptions that accompany changes.[4] However, this characteristic, which has served to make one a successful change leader, has the drawback of making it difficult for one to understand why some librarians and staff members have difficulty adjusting to the idea of change and supporting new endeavors or initiatives. This chapter will draw on some of the basic literature from the world of psychology to explain typical responses to change and offer suggestions on how to manage the impact of personalized emotional responses to change on organizational initiatives.

A DIFFERENCE IN PERSPECTIVE

For most managers or leaders, the changes they initiate represent an obvious opportunity for something positive where the institution gains something. These gains can be easily reported to staff as a result of the change. Sometimes the gain may be measurable, such as a budget savings that allows other cuts to be avoided or recovered money reallocated. Other changes have highly visible benefits, such as new furnishings or a major physical renovation in a worn-out building. Even if there have been mistakes in design or implementation, there is still a clearer understanding of the reason behind the change and the overall benefit from enacting the change. Sometimes a change occurs in response to a negative event, such as a financial shortfall. But even in this situation, the impetus for change challenges leaders and employees at all levels to find a way to make lemonade when handed lemons. In these cases the purpose or value of the change can be understood by all stakeholders and the results appreciated across the board.

Organizational structure or workflow changes are different and face significant challenges for staff in understanding the benefits of the change. Work space reconfigurations can fall into the category of either a perceived positive or negative based on the initiating cause. New, stylish furniture for all is usually a visible positive, unless it is accompanied by significant reapportionment of one's personal space where some employees end up with smaller work surfaces or space. However, workflow or organizational restructuring-driven rearrangements can be a manifestation of the earlier operational, service, or space changes and will often emulate or revitalize the emotions associated with that change. Similarly, taking forward changes that address the ideological role and core services of librarianship can be even more difficult than internal shuffling. Addressing these challenges through targeted communication techniques and implementation timelines is addressed in subsequent chapters. But in order to know how to communicate and plan effectively for success, it is important for the leader to understand how a front-line employee's perspective on the proposed change is different from that of the person leading it.

COMMON MANAGERIAL ASSUMPTIONS

It is a common but risky practice for managers to think they understand an individual and to assign standard categories or reasons to an individual's act of change resistance. Even as one may think one understands another individual, unless one can mirror the other person's life experiences with a similar emotional style, one cannot truly intuit knowledge of another. That said, many managers will often make assumptions about why an individual resists a change initiative, based on what they do know of an individual and the individual's behavior or actions. The following theories represent some common assumptions manifested by managers to explain an employee's perspective on resisting change. If one is accurate and respectful in one's understanding, it can give one insights for communicating further with the individual and gaining buy-in. However, if one has misdiagnosed the change-resistant motivation, it will actually damage the professional relationship and seriously undermine the success of future change initiatives.

The authors identified five viewpoints of managerial assumptions on why employees resist change from the literature.[5] It is not uncommon to have each of these perspectives represented by one or more individuals in a large organization. Even though they are seen to be competing motivations for change resistance, an employee or manager may assign complex combinations of the different philosophies in a single individual. This is most probable when one is dealing with sweeping change that impacts an organization at multiple levels, thereby triggering a destabilizing combination of change-reactive responses. In looking at each of these perspectives, one may be able to better classify the source of an emotional or behavioral response. It is important to realize that these perspectives represent assumptions and conclusions reached by the manager and may or may not be accurate for the individual.

Kotter and Schlesinger outline the first four competing perspectives, which tend to reflect a more patriarchal or hierarchical thinking on the part of the manager. [6] They believe that the "parochial self-interest perspective" is one of the most common reasons why employees resist change. The foundation of the parochial self-interest perspective rests on the belief that employees are resistant to change based solely out of their own self-interest and care little about the success of the overall organization. However, managers who tend to attribute resistance to change of their employees to this perspective are highly judgmental, distrusting, and critical of their own employees. Though they often do not realize it, the change managers become the reason why change is resisted instead of the catalyst to propel change.

A second managerial perspective on change resistance revolves around the belief by managers that their employees simply misunderstand the reason for the change and this is what leads them to resist change. These managers believe that the solution to their employees' misunderstanding problem is that they as leaders need to communicate better with their employees so that they receive the information they need to understand the necessary change. This model suggests that if communication was increased so that the employees understood the change, then employees' resistance to change would be conquered. Unfortunately, this tends to focus more on top-down communication rather than on interactive inquiry-based communication to actually understand the employees' position. What change managers forget is that most employees understand what their job responsibilities and duties are better than their managers do because the employee is doing the job daily with all its situational exceptions. As a result, employees are better equipped to understand the effect change will have on them, and no amount of increased communication or saying it with different words will necessarily alter the way they view the impact of the change on their positions.

The third reason managers believe employees resist change is called the "different assessments perspective." This theory, although similar to the misunderstanding perspective, rests on the belief that not every employee will agree with what the change manager communicates as the benefits or advantages of change. As a result, before change can be achieved, both management and employees affected by the change will need to communicate these differences of beliefs and adopt a common set. Due to this communication component, the different assessment perspective often develops into the misunderstanding perspective because most managers are so committed to the "rightness" of their beliefs that they believe that adoption of their belief as the common one can be conquered simply through increased communication.

The fourth change-resistance perspective which Kotter and Schlesinger point to attributes resistance to an individual having a low tolerance to change.[7] This change model rests on the foundation that some employees have higher security and stability needs than other employees. Consequently, these employees will be more resistant to change, and if a manager wants to achieve change, the only way will be to address the security needs of these employees.

An alternative change-resistance perspective is called the "competing commitment to change." According to Cervone, many change-resistance cases do not fall into any of the above four change perspective theories because they "do not adequately explain or help resolve issues related to change resistance."[8] Kegan and Lehey argue that the reason why employees resist change is because they have competing commitments and values toward the proposed change which act collectively to create change resistance.[9] Successful change managers can help employees overcome and conquer their resistance to change by creating a work environment that helps them acknowledge and understand their competing commitments. However, it is important that the change manager not assume that recognizing and understanding competing commitments can be achieved overnight. In addition, some employees in the process of uncovering their competing commitments may begin to question their fundamental beliefs and activities, which can be part of an individual's identity.

A perfect example of competing commitments can be seen where a subject bibliographer begins requesting the library to start purchasing graphic novels or photographic material of the human body for the first time. Employees throughout the technical services and shelving workflows may be put off at handling these materials based on their personal opinion of the value of the material. They begin questioning why the library is buying "this type of material." Often the books are pulled out of the normal workflow and are brought to various managers by those employees who don't believe that the library should be purchasing "this type of material" because they see it as being inappropriate for the library collection. According to Cervone, "Often people will have to confront beliefs held since childhood or admit to harboring feelings that are either painful or embarrassing. Nonetheless, it is by exposing these beliefs that we are able to recognize the contradictions in our lives, move on, and adapt."[10] While still introducing a stereotyping risk, this latter perspective recognizes a more mature and engaged employee who is struggling to adapt to change on a fundamental level and where open-minded, engaged communication can play a better role in overcoming change resistance.

ADDRESSING CHANGE-RESISTANT EMPLOYEES

"Change-resistant employees." Every organization has them, and leaders often choose to deal with them in different ways depending on one's managerial perspective on the reason for the resistance, career experience, and personal style of leadership. Many managers with a more traditional leadership style may resonate with Kotter and Schlesinger and basically override employee objections in the name of progress and tell them to just get over it and get on board. At an extreme, this will be the manager or administrator who publicly announces that anyone who does not like the idea is welcome to find somewhere else to work or who works to actively marginalize dissenters within the organization by reduced autonomy in carrying out one's job or applying negative labels. According to Tvedt, Saksvik, and Nytro, if leaders brush aside the change-resistant employees under the assumption that they are being "irrational," then these leaders do not realize that doing this can make matters worse.[11] One of the key factors of this approach is that it works without a significant impact on the change initiative so long as the change resisters represent a small part of the overall employee base and they do not engender respect or excessive sympathy from their peers for their position. However, in situations where the change resisters represent a larger part of the employee base or are perceived as grassroots leaders, this approach can turn ugly and significantly undermine the long-term success of the initiative. This is a perfect example of how poor leadership practice fails to properly address the reason why people are resistant to change, and if anything this practice helps to reinforce and entrench resistance to change.[12] In other words, the major reason why organizations fail to implement change quickly is because change leaders do not anticipate and address the human aspects side of change.[13]

Within the organizational power structure, change resisters generally do not have the political strength to prevent change, but there is an organizational penalty to the more dictatorial approach. At best, employees are disaffected for a time until they have managed to work through the emotions associated with the change and/or the benefits of the change are more visible to all. Change resisters may deliberately employ passive resistance in preparing for the change, engaging in the planning, or seeking out barriers to delay the change, hoping that the proposed change will get overtaken by events and become a lower priority or get canceled. While this usually will not stop the change, it will slow it down and leave residual follow-up that must be addressed by the manager when the next change comes along. At worst, these employees can develop a truly toxic attitude toward the change and act in a way that undermines or sabotages the benefits of the change and actually damages the organization. Subsequently, the latter will often trigger negative evaluations or disciplinary procedures that have employees taking sides and require tremendous energies on the manager's part to resolve, all diminishing the positive progress or impact of the change initiative.

Another alternate approach in keeping with more contemporary business models of shared investment, engagement, and empowerment is to implement change in a way that provides employees an opportunity to work through their emotions, beliefs, and values about the change and for managers and leaders to respond to the emotion-based communications in a more positive and constructive way. In this situation, the employee feels supported throughout the change and will engage more effectively to move the change forward because understanding and reason will reduce the emotional drag. In order to adopt this approach the manager or leader needs to understand what these underlying emotions are and what the natural cycle is in dealing with a change. One core issue is that for most staff, the change is being enacted upon them rather than their having initiated the change.[14] From this perspective, it is automatically their perception that the change creates a situation of diminished control where the front-line employee is going to have to give up something. This something may be specific like a favorite task or a workflow the employee had invested in, or it may be vague like a loss of free time, an expectation to work more intensely or efficiently, or a sense of loss of organizational support. The manager taking this path must be flexible and engage in negotiation as a part of building positive momentum to support the change through true empowerment and recognition of front-line expert knowledge.[15]

Even when using the latter approach, there may be individuals who, from their own personal life experiences, cannot deal well with change until it is fully enacted upon them with blatantly obvious benefits. No matter how much communication, engagement, and empowerment a leader employs, they are never going to be in favor of change. For these individuals, the directive approach is the only feasible one to employ. However, by the time the leader has to take on the more heavy-handed role, one will have used the engagement approach to build a strong ally base of the employee's peers and possibly even subordinates to all help the resister accept the change. At this point, the overall organizational morale will stay positive and the change will move through with negligible effect on the resister's part. Specific approaches and techniques are provided in later chapters on actual change planning and implementation.

One final caution about responding to change-resistant employees: should a manager or leader encounter change resistance outside the norm, then it is critical to step back from the change and question the approach one is using in leading the change across the organization. One abnormal manifestation of change resistance is when the employees resisting the change are librarians and staff who are normally in favor of change. Another red flag is when the change-resistant employees are those who are generally seen as organizational leaders and the ones who speak up for others. Finally, leaders should be concerned if a large percentage of the impacted unit is against the change after having had time to give it some thought and move through the denial stage (which is discussed in the next section). All of these are indicative of a problem in either how the change is being presented or in the core assumptions driving the change initiative.

STAGES OF CHANGE ADJUSTMENT

As shown in the Kubler-Ross model, there are generally four stages individuals go through in accepting the impact that a change has on them personally: denial, resistance, exploration, commitment.[16] However, the amount of time spent in each stage can vary situationally and from person to person. Also, while the process is normally one where someone progresses through the stages in a linear fashion, it is possible for an individual to need to revisit the different stages as the actual change unfolds. During the denial stage an individual is still responding to the event from a state of shock, disbelief, or numbness.[17] The resistance stage is where the strongest emotions are manifested and is where many people get stuck. They quit thinking and move to a state of emotional reacting. This can be the hardest state to break through because the individuals are often not using their own active listening skills but are hearing comments with personal filters of anger, hurt, loss, doubt, and distrust. Most employees will eventually move past the resistance stage and into the exploration phase. This is where they have accepted to need to engage on the change at one level but there is still a period of personal development, adjustment, and questioning. For some, this may be the period when they are learning new skills or working within a new framework. Finally, employees will enter the stage of commitment. As the name implies, this is where the employee has reengaged and bought into the change and is now directing one's focus and energies to make it successful. Sometimes the commitment stage will manifest itself as more of a grudging acceptance than active engagement, and it is only through time that the acceptance will truly morph into true engagement.[18]

Even as this describes the basic cycle an individual goes through, it is possible for someone to be juggling several change cycles simultaneously or even to be coping with nested changes that are all at different stages of the adjustment process. For example, suppose Helen is an interlibrary loan-processing clerk in the Smith Library. Six weeks ago Margaret, the longtime head of access services (including circulation and interlibrary services), announced her sudden retirement. After considering the issue of replacing Margaret, library administrators decide that they are going to restructure the department and give some promising librarians the opportunity to advance into management. Interlibrary services will get a new department head, Kevin, and will relocate to an office suite on the third floor. Circulation will stay on the first floor and get Allison as its new department head. Both Kevin and Allison are from different units of the library, electronic resource acquisitions and reference respectively. So now Helen, normally a fairly resilient and level-headed employee, is trying to adjust to no longer working near her friends from circulation, to having a new and different cubicle that is configured totally differently than her old desk area, and, last but not least, to figuring out a new manager's communication style and expectations for success. Add in that the administration would like Kevin to implement a new book-paging service that will require some significant new work tasks by Helen. What you have is a formula for overreactions from anyone dealing with such an accumulated emotional barrage. Taken independently, Helen could probably work through the change cycle with minimal stress or workplace impact. However, the cumulative effect has taken away her buffer zones to where she feels pushed from all sides with no support system in place, and Kevin should not be surprised when she overreacts to his next change suggestion.

PERSONALIZING THE CHANGE

For change to be the most successful, employees and managers must invest in the change at a personal level.[19] This is why organizations that develop a true culture surrounding their vision and are effective in having employees take ownership of the vision are most successful and seem to be more effective at implementing positive change. Everyone has bought into believing in the message as having value to them and being part of their workplace identity, which is also in harmony with their personal goals and value system. However, there are two sides to this coin. The employee that has most bought in to the philosophy may have the strongest personal response against an action one perceives as going against this core vision, almost to the point of an ethical dilemma.[20] This can be particularly problematic in an environment where employees are encouraged to build engaged personal relationships centered on teamwork.

In addition to strong reactions based on accumulated multidimensional changes as described earlier in the chapter, employees can bog down on a change when the issues resonate at an intensely personal level and conflict with their core values or self-identity in their jobs. In this sort of situation, the change may actually be more reflective of a bereavement situation and the individuals will be going through a manifestation of the grief process, with an accompanying sense of loss of something very important to them or abandonment by the organization. Change that has a lot of emotion behind it can also trigger a response that is similar to a post-traumatic stress event. An employee who went through a reduction-in-force situation, either as an individual who was laid off or a post-layoff "survivor," may have an extremely strong emotional reaction to any budget-tightening initiatives. Suppose a library employee, Kristina, had previously worked in a small business environment where her male supervisor made inappropriate comments to the point where she felt forced to leave work she enjoyed doing and went through a difficult time financially while trying to find a new job. Now, several years later, she is told that the female supervisor she enjoys working under is being reassigned and her new supervisor is a male with a superficial resemblance to the previous problem supervisor in age, height, general build, and so on. The department head does not understand why Kristina, who is normally an employee who responds positively to change, is suddenly having difficulties adjusting to the situation and seems to be scared and distrustful of the new supervisor.

Even for the scenario described earlier with Helen, many change leaders would have difficulty understanding why the change is difficult for her. What they do not realize is how strong a personal association an individual can form to some aspect of the workplace. Many employees whose work revolves around routine tasks have difficulty connecting their daily job responsibilities with the greater good or mission of the library. These individuals will find other aspects of their work environment to satisfy the need to establish their work identity connections. This may be through status symbols, such as the size or condition of one's work area. It can also be through the relationships they have built with coworkers. Similarly, resources can be a function of their value to the organization, such as who gets the new computers or the office closest to the window or break room. Professional librarians are not immune to this effect. As traditional library services seem to go by the wayside with new technologies and expectations of users, some push back as they feel the profession they had invested in is now leaving them behind, and the values of accurate information through the catalog or reference interview and the teaching of critical research skills disappear in favor of the immediate gratification of a handful of full-text articles easily accessed through a Google-like interface.

Another aspect of personalization occurs when employees are required to make radical changes to or dismantle a process that they put a significant amount of effort into developing. In the past, a workflow or process might be static or only tweaked slightly for a number of years. Even when subsequent adjustments were made, they were more of an incremental approach. This is no longer the case. The rate of environmental change and necessary response to technology stimuli are forcing all organizations, including libraries, to change at ever-increasing rates to keep up. Instead of implementing change in an incremental way, current management and leadership philosophy seems to be preaching the TNT approach of blowing up the old in favor of a radically different new. Organizations subject their employees to rapid and drastic organizational changes that affect the position's responsibilities and cause these employees to be faced with new pressures, expectations, and demands. For the employee, these pressures cause increasing workplace stress and poor job performance, which end up costing the organization considerable amounts of money and decrease the overall morale of the organization's employees.[21] As a positive, this approach immediately pushes employees outside their comfort zone to a totally new way of thinking about a process or service and can move the organization forward in a way that an incremental change approach will never match. As a negative, it can leave employees who invested in a process devastated by the cavalier dismissal of their past effort and floundering to find something familiar to hold on to. Again, there is a sense on the employee's part of losing something of personal value or validation in the "new way."

EMOTIONAL ENGAGEMENT

So what are the emotions employees experience as they are trying to adjust to a change? In truth, few employees get enthusiastic and excited about having their work environment tipped on its head, even when they can see a positive result down the road. Change managers know that although employees need to become accustomed to organizational change, the change process can be difficult, particularly when the change is drastic.[22] Often there is an element of stoic endurance for the forthcoming hardships of learning new skills, being displaced during construction, or just getting behind in one's work while participating in the planning that goes into developing a new workflow. Another theme that was mentioned earlier is a sense of loss that can be accompanied by varying levels of bereavement or grief.[23] Change managers can alleviate some of the pressure caused by stress if they focus on their employees in addition to change strategy.[24] One study done by Lohela and others found that one of the factors that increased an employee's risk of a negative change in health was driven by a negative change in job stress.[25] Furthermore, the study showed that better organizational leadership could increase the chance of positive changes in an employee's health.[26] Obviously, a healthier employee will be more engaged and a positive influence on the workplace. Another intense emotional response can develop when employees feel that they or their value system are under attack because of the change. Due to this de-motivated feeling among employees, there has been an increasing amount of research around work values and the importance of complementary values among the employee, supervisor, and the rest of the organization.[27] In this emotional mindset, employees can feel victimized or powerless.[28] Unfortunately, there is no simple magic wand a leader or manager can wave to make the emotions follow a prescribed pattern or go away. However, according to Kanter, employees can be energized in their position by being engaged in problem solving and mobilized for change by their involvement in a participative structure that permits them to venture beyond their normal work roles to tackle meaningful issues.[29]

MANAGER AS COUNSELOR—MAYBE?

There are several factors under a manager's control that can influence an individual's level of emotional response to a change. The first is to avoid the personalization trap that the employee is in and maintain a professional detachment toward the issue. If the managers take employees' natural resistance or anger to the change personally and start interacting with employees at an emotional level, feeling a need to be defensive or angry at the lack of support, the situation will deteriorate rapidly. One can support and lead a change without having made it a part of one's leadership identity, and in fact doing so will force one to look at the change more thoughtfully and analytically and have the answers to the questions that others are asking. This latter approach can be most challenging for intuitive leaders who "feel" a change is best but cannot explain it. While managers find it frustrating that others are not on board, channeling these frustrations back to the individual will lead to a breakdown in communication that can seriously hamper the success of the initiative. Patience, not overreacting, and a willingness to be flexible on the details are some of the most important skills in the manager's toolkit for leading change.

Another technique for addressing the emotional side of leading change is to pace the planning and implementation in a way that provides time for emotional adjustment to the change by as many employees as possible. It may be a cliché but is not inaccurate to tell someone who has experienced a loss that time will heal it. The same is true for staging out changes in the organization when one is aware that employees feel they are having to let go of something or experiencing a sense of loss, in addition to being moved outside of their comfort zone. This can be difficult for many managers, whose clear-sighted enthusiasm and confidence about an idea will lead them to want to move forward with a full implementation immediately. In truth this often fosters a false perspective of the urgency of the change and can lead to distrust and loss of confidence on the part of the staff.

For employees experiencing a sense of victimization or feelings of being power-less, the best thing a manager can do is to give them an opportunity to be a part of the decision-making process. Unfortunately, many managers shy away from this because they feel that including naysayers undermines the progress of a change or encourages others to challenge their own leadership authority. They would rather compose the implementation team with individuals who have already bought into the change to move it along more smoothly and quickly. In actuality, this only defers the conflict for another day and actually feeds into the conspiracy theory mindset of employees who are already feeling disenfranchised. Though it takes more time up front and may actually require managers to rethink their timetable, engaging with these employees earlier will actually create a more successful implementation at the end. Additionally, if one can look past employees' emotional fears, there may be valid contributions embedded in their concerns that need to be incorporated into the plan. This is discussed in more detail in chapters 4 and 5.

Another thing that a manager can do is to encourage some techniques that are actually used in therapy. Middle managers and project leaders should focus on active listening with an open mind rather than directing based on the view from the top. This gives employees the chance to have their voices heard and gives them the opportu-nity to work through a train of thought in understanding the change. Additionally, a manager should not feel the need to immediately respond to or counter employees' comments or conclusions. Doing so actually gives employees the impression that they are not being heard. Instead, use active listening techniques to come to agreement on what issues are most troubling to the employee and take the issues away for thought on the best way to address them. After looking at the framework of the change with the concerns in mind, get back to the employee with a personal response. Even if one has to tell employees that one is not making a change based on their input, the employees have had their day in court, which is often an aspect of moving past the victim's emotions. Another technique for diminishing victimization is to encourage these employees to talk with peers across the organization about the change and build a support network, akin to group therapy. The latter is actually difficult for many managers because they perceive this conduct in the context of a grassroots rebellion that undermines the change effort. In actuality, listening to a peer complain about a situation and realizing how it *really* comes across can lead someone else to avoid such close-minded, unbecoming behavior. Similarly, peer pressure to accept a change is a powerful motivator, and shutting down the grapevine also shuts down the leader's allies and supporters who might be in a position to lend the voice of reason to conversations. If what the manager fears does occur, that the victimized employee is effective in stirring up a rebellion to the change, it is a sign that there are serious problems with overall organizational support of the change and the manager should pause and reassess the entire goal of the change.

So how might one address some of these suggested techniques? For example, suppose Tim is a cataloger who asks for a meeting to tell you he is unhappy about loading a particular set of records purchased from a vendor into the catalog because he has heard that the records are not up to an acceptable standard. When you meet with him, actually engage in dialogue about what the specific things are about the records that are substandard. Ask for alternate ideas to still accomplish the overall goal that the records would support. Then tell Tim he has given you things to think about and thank him for coming by, which probably took a lot of courage on his part. After taking his concerns into consideration, rather than publicly announce an override decision to do it anyway, take a few minutes to meet with Tim or send him an e-mail. In this communication validate that his concerns have merit. Confirm what is accurate about his concerns, such as the fact that the purchased records are not up to the same standard as the other records in the catalog. Then depersonalize the decision by mentioning how introducing these records does not undermine the overall integrity of the catalog, and outline what benefits come from making an exception and loading them. At this point you can say that you feel that the benefits, *in this situation*, outweigh the negatives and that you have made the decision to go ahead and approve the records to be loaded. Finally, close with an encouragement for Tim to speak up and be a part of future decisions. At this point, Tim knows his advice was not followed, but he also knows that his concerns were listened to and he has not been labeled a "problem employee" by speaking up.

For situations where managers and employees have a strong rapport and generally positive history and the employee is uncomfortable in adjusting to the change but may not be at a level of rage or despair to warrant a referral to the employee assistance program, the manager may want to try to understand the underlying emotional motivation that the employee is struggling with and address it through engagement and communication with the employee. It may be that the issues the employee sees as problems were ones the manager truly overlooked or miscommunicated, or the manager may have already considered and resolved them. Finally, for those employees having the most difficulty, encourage them to make use of employee assistance program resources in developing their resiliency in adjusting and adapting to change. This may be particularly useful if the individual's resiliency to changes in the workplace is being exacerbated by issues at home that are totally outside the control of the manager. It may also allow the individual to better understand and compartmentalize the frustrations and thereby improve one's ability to bring one's concerns to the table for clarification and engaged discussion. This helps to keep the manager from being cast in the true therapist role and, for a situation such as the one described earlier with Kristina, puts her in the hands of someone who can help her work through her own issues overflowing into the situation.

The worst thing for a change leader to do is to dismiss the emotions as not having validity or importance. This effectively marginalizes the employees along with their feelings and positions the leader as an insensitive dictator. This is a particularly problematic approach in libraries where one is dealing with a recognized professional attitude and perspective on the part of degreed and experienced librarians and a frequently feminine communication style. Recognizing the emotions and being willing to address their impact goes a long way to making the change a more positive, less negative event.

KEYS TO SUCCESS

This chapter introduces a lot of information that challenges leaders and managers to rethink how they perceive change resistance in employees. The models presented are not the only ones that can be found in the various literature of psychology or sociology, but they are ones that resonated with the authors as particularly relevant to libraries as organizational environments, often with traditional administrative hierarchical structures.

- The most important thing for a change leader or manager to recognize is the importance of understanding that there may be different reasons why individuals react to change the way they do and that these reasons may be personal.
- When concerns become personal with a person's sense of values or ethics involved, that person has the potential to become volatile and committed to resist the change and undermine the success of the change initiative.
- It is critical to be careful if one is making assumptions about why an employee is resisting change and avoid stereotypes that project an authoritarian or elitist-based approach.
- In such a highly emotional scenario, a manager who is leading change is challenged to have highly developed skills in communicating effectively, particularly in employing listening skills with patience and empathy, as well as explaining the reason behind the change initiative.
- Even as the change may be personal to the employee, the change leader should maintain a level of personal detachment when the change initiative

is resisted or attacked in order to be open to hearing employee concerns and giving them appropriate consideration and/or validation.

THINKING EXERCISES

1. Think of times you have disagreed with something someone suggested you do, and the emotions you experienced. What were they? Were they different depending on whether the person was a direct report, peer manager, or administrator?

2. Suppose you had to tell your department they are moving into a different office area that is much less convenient for them. How do you think they would react and why?

3. Think of a major operational change you could make in your unit (for the purpose of the exercise, it does not need to be feasible in terms of budget). Who are your knowledge experts in the area? Who are other stakeholders that would be impacted by the change? What techniques would you use to address different emotion-based responses to the change for optimal buy-in?

4. Think about the last time you tried to lead a change and someone resisted it. Think about how you felt about the person's resistance. Which of the managerial assumptions on change-resistance perspectives described earlier in the chapter were being manifested?

NOTES

1. Gina Gotsill and Meryl Natchez, "From Resistance to Acceptance: How to Implement Change Management." *T+D*, November 2007.
2. Donald E. Riggs, "What's in Store for Academic Libraries? Leadership and Management Issues," *Journal of Academic Librarianship* 23 (January 1997): 3–7.
3. Gotsill and Natchez, "From Resistance to Acceptance."
4. Wade H. Shaw, "Celebrating the Leadership of Peter F. Drucker," *IEEE Engineering Management Review* 34, no. 2 (2006): 2.
5. H. Frank Cervone, "Working through Resistance to Change by Using the Competing Commitments Model," *International Digital Library Perspectives* 23, no. 3 (2007): 250–53.
6. John P. Kotter and Leonard A. Schlesinger, "Choosing Strategies for Change," *Harvard Business Review* (March–April 1979): 106–14.
7. Ibid.
8. Cervone, "Working through Resistance to Change."

9. Robert Kegan and Lisa Laskow Lehey, "The Real Reason People Won't Change," *Harvard Business Review* (November 2001): 85–92.
10. Cervone, "Working through Resistance to Change."
11. Sturle D. Tvedt, Per Oystein Saksvik, and Kjell Nytro, "Does Change Process Healthiness Reduce the Negative Effects of Organizational Change on the Psychosocial Work Environment?" *Work and Stress* 23 (January–March 2009): 80–98.
12. Michael Hammer and Steven Stanton, *The Reengineering Revolution: A Handbook* (New York: HarperBusiness, 1995).
13. Olivera Majanovic, "Supporting the 'Soft' Side of Business Process Reengineering," *Business Process Management Journal* 6, no. 1 (2000): 43–55.
14. Ibid.
15. Ibid.
16. Elisabeth Kubler-Ross, *On Death and Dying* (New York: Macmillan, 1969).
17. Ibid.
18. Ibid.
19. Sally Woodward and Chris Hendry, "Leading and Coping with Change," *Journal of Change Management* 4 (June 2004): 155–83.
20. Jennifer Dose, "Work Values: An Integrative Framework and Illustrative Application to Organizational Socialization," *Journal of Occupational and Organizational Psychology* 70 (1997): 219–40.
21. Confederation of British Industry, *The Lost Billions: Annual Healthcare Survey of Absence and Turnover 2002* (London: Confederation of British Industry/AXA PPP Healthcare, 2003).
22. N. Nicholson, "The Transition Cycle: Causes, Outcomes, Processes, and Forms," in *On the Move: The Psychology of Change and Transition*, ed. S. Fisher and C. L. Cooper (London: John Wiley and Sons, 1990); William Bridges, *Managing Transitions: Making the Most of Change*, 2nd ed. (Cambridge, MA: Perseus, 2003).
23. Kubler-Ross, *On Death and Dying.*
24. Woodward and Hendry, "Leading and Coping with Change."
25. Malin Lohela and others, "Does a Change in Psychosocial Work Factors Lead to a Change in Employee Health?" *Journal of Occupational and Environmental Medicine* 51, no. 2 (2009): 195–203.
26. Lohela and others (2009); Per Oystein Saksvik and others, "Developing Criteria for Healthy Organizational Change," *Work and Stress* 21 (July-September, 2007): 243–63.
27. Bruce Meglino, Elizabeth Ravlin, and Cheryl Adkins, "Value Congruence and Satisfaction with a Leader: An Examination of the Role of Interaction," *Human Relations* 44 (May 1991): 481–95; Martha A. Brown, "Values—A Necessary but Neglected Ingredient of Motivation on the Job," *Academy of Management Review* 1 (October 1976): 12–23.
28. Jennifer Dose, "Work Values: An Integrative Framework and Illustrative Application to Organizational Socialization," *Journal of Occupational and Organizational Psychology* 70 (1997): 219–40.
29. Rosabeth Moss Kanter and Barry Stein, *The Challenge of Organizational Change: How Companies Experience It and Leaders Guide It* (New York: Free Press; Toronto: Maxwell Macmillan Canada; New York: Maxwell Macmillan International, 1992).

CHAPTER THREE

ORGANIZATIONAL CULTURE IMPACT

Some are born great, some achieve greatness,
and some have greatness thrust upon 'em.

—Shakespeare, *Twelfth Night*

WHEN DEALING WITH institutional changes, the current organizational culture can have a huge impact on predicting the success of a change initiative. It can act in a way that supports or undermines the change. Even as managers or leaders may not have been active in establishing the current organizational culture, they will need to be cautious of the impact that their own initiatives will have on the organization's culture or vice versa. Organization culture is an extremely complex issue for libraries because it develops based on events over a period of time and involving the personalized interactions of many individuals. For academic libraries, it may also be a function of the greater institutional culture. Changing organizational culture is a particularly challenging type of change and is discussed later in this chapter. More often, a leader or manager will be executing a change in the context of a preestablished or transitioning organizational culture. In this situation, understanding the organizational culture is an important part of developing the implementation plan and anticipating trigger points that can spark or quash a change initiative.

WHAT IS ORGANIZATIONAL CULTURE?

The foundation on which any society rests is its culture. How people dress, the types of food they eat, the language they use, the values they believe in, the way they behave, and even the music they listen to is all dictated by the shared culture they live in. However, the impact culture has on a group goes beyond a societal phenomenon. Martin stresses that organizations, regardless of their size, also have a culture.[1] Edgar Schein, who is considered the father of organization culture, defines organizational culture as "a pattern of shared basic assumptions that the group learned as it solved its problems of external adaptation and internal integration, that has worked well enough to be considered valid and therefore, to be taught to new members as the correct way to perceive, think, and feel in relation to those problems."[2] It is the culture of an organization rather than structure, strategy, or politics that is the prime mover in the organization.[3]

IMPORTANCE OF ORGANIZATIONAL CULTURE

An organization often develops its culture around practices or levels. According to Jordan, there are three primary levels that exist in all organizations.[4] These can be summarized as follows:

Individual level—where the employee's main motivator is to meet the wishes of her boss. The employee's experience with her boss or even other employees forms the basis of the employee's experiences with the organizational culture, and this is why organizational culture rests on the personal element.

Group level—where the manager's main motivator is to focus on relationships among her employees and the need to formulate a group identity. In libraries a culture can form around groups of employees at a departmental level, such as a cataloging culture or reference culture. In addition, a culture can also develop around a particular workflow or function, such as forgiving fines.

Organization level—where the goal of the CEO is to build a smooth and efficient organization and establish the purpose of the organization and assessment in accomplishing set goals.

Strong organizational culture gives people a sense of pride in what they do for the organization, and this sense of pride leads them to more than likely work harder. Deal and Kennedy believe that a strong culture is preferable to a weak culture because it reduces workplace uncertainty by having a system of informal rules that spell out to employees what is acceptable work behavior.[5] In order for an organization to be strong, the goals of the organization level must be achieved. However, the only way to achieve the goals of the organization level is to first achieve the goals of the individual and group levels. Problems arise when an employee is not properly motivated or if a team is having trouble working together; then the individual and group levels cannot be achieved and the organization as a whole will be negatively affected, causing a weak organizational culture.[6] Deal and Kennedy believe there are five elements that drive organizational cultures to be strong or weak.[7] These are summarized in the following manner.

1. *Organizational environment* is the manner in which the organization has to be responsive to the external environment and generally is the most influential element that shapes an organization's culture. If an organization is to succeed in business it must operate according to the needs of that market, not to the needs of the organization. In libraries, a perfect example of this is the often heated debate over electronic vs. print materials. Some libraries struggle with electronic materials because of licensing and updating challenges and overall increased costs. However, as more library patrons expect items to be accessible electronically, if the library organization does not listen to its market then the market will search for alternative forms to gain its information needs. As a result, libraries will be seen by patrons as unnecessary and obsolete.

2. *Organizational cultural values* are the fundamental concepts and beliefs of an organization that are directly related to the established standards of achievement for employees within the organization. It is these values that define for the employees if the organization is successful or not. For libraries a fundamental belief might be that "we meet the needs of all our users." However, if an organizational change occurs, such as the merging of key public service desks with minimal or rushed training, then the fundamental concept of the organization is seen by employees to be compromised. As a result, the cultural values of the organization are undermined, creating a weaker organizational culture.

3. *Organizational heroes* are those employees who embody the cultural value of the organization and who can act as role models for other employees within the organization. The problem with organizational heroes is they are individuals with their own opinions. What this means is if you have an employee who is seen by your department as the organizational hero and this employee agrees with the change, it significantly

strengthens support for the change. However, the hero may disagree with the proposed change. If the organizational hero disagrees "in public" with the manager, then the culture of the organization is damaged, thereby creating a weaker organizational culture. (Working with local heroes as grassroots leaders and as sources of feedback about the change is discussed in later chapters.)

4. *Organizational rites and rituals* are the systematic and normal routine of everyday life in the organization. If everyone within the organization has different rites and rituals then there is nothing tying the organization together, thereby creating a weaker organizational culture. These can include major rites and rituals such as an annual longevity ceremony and minor rituals such as established norms in scheduling and lunch breaks. Conflicts in organizational rites and rituals further weaken an organizational culture, such as one department being "required" to take a lunch break and another department being "allowed" the individual flexibility to work a shorter day and skip lunch.

5. *The organizational cultural network* is the informal means of communication that takes place within the organization. It is this informal communication network that carries the corporate values and heroic mythology to all employees. Some managers view this network in a negative way as the office grapevine, but like the organizational hero, this network builds background support among peers or prepares employees for a change initiative. However, it can damage the culture of the organization by consistently communicating negative, contradictory, and/or incorrect information to the organization's employees.

It is important to remember that if the organization fails to adapt to its environment and relies on only one particular manifestation of its organizational culture, such as the rites and rituals, the organization will fail. Similarly, trying to disavow or marginalize an aspect of the organizational culture, such as the network, will increase the likelihood that a change initiative will fail.

Studying organizational culture is a complex task that is not without controversy. Some management perspectives prefer to downplay the role of organizational culture, feeling that the command approach is sufficient. Others take organizational culture to extremes by deliberately, or even aggressively, creating a groupthink model through behavioral hiring and training. Most contemporary libraries fall somewhere in the middle between these two extremes. The growing emphasis on customer service has led many libraries to adopt environment-driven organizational values, which as stated above play into the development of a culture. In addition, libraries have traditionally been an environment with limited turnover and department structures laden with experienced staff. It is often the senior staff members who perpetuate organizational culture, though it may be modified by validated input from newer staff members. The anticipated increase in retirements on the part of the baby boomer generation may result in more flexibility and changes within the organizational culture.

Many change leaders become frustrated in working around or through organizational culture in trying to implement a major change initiative. However, if a manager wants to implement change in the organization, one must first understand the culture of the organization, including its values, heroes, rituals, and networks, to effect appropriate actions. Morgan goes one step further by stating that the "single most important factor" between an organization's success and failure is the need to understand its organizational culture.[8]

TYPES OF ORGANIZATIONAL CULTURE

In the literature there are a variety of names used to describe the four types of cultures that resonate in today's organizations. However, for the purpose of introducing concepts in the context of libraries and this book, we will use Hendy's four examples of organizational cultures: person, task, power, and role.[9] Each of these is described below.

1. A *person culture* is where the employees see themselves as the fundamental positions in the organization and the organizational structure exists only to support those individuals. These individuals feel little if any loyalty to the organization but instead see the organization as a place to do their own thing.[10] Taken to extremes, this type of organizational culture becomes dysfunctional because the needs of the individual are placed over the needs of the organization. As a result the performance of work is hindered.

2. A *task culture* occurs when the employees are job- or project-oriented. In this type of organizational culture, employers bring the best-qualified, highly motivated people together to get a task done. These employees generally need little to no supervision and use the best resources and methods for achieving their task. Once one task is completed the group

moves on to the next assigned task. Problems arise when members of the group become competitive and forget the object of the task, instead shifting their focus to a person-culture perspective of their own promotion or recognition. It can also be problematic when employees or groups feel that their "tasks" are not given the same value or importance in the organization that they feel should be the case.

3. A *power culture* depends on a centralized power leader for its organization to succeed. Usually, for this culture to be successful, a charismatic individual leader responds quickly, decisively, and unilaterally with the best intentions for the organization in mind. However, these types of leaders can be very demanding on their employees, and the organization can become inefficient because employees must wait for approval from the leader before moving forward on an idea. This culture can become dysfunctional if the leader is not sufficiently charismatic, but instead uses threats or other dictatorial approaches in defending poor decisions. Another pitfall that puts this culture in conflict with a task culture is that ideas which are not seen by the leader as "good ideas" are dismissed without proper consideration. Employees within this type of organizational culture often become resentful that their experience is not being utilized, and they burn out. Similarly, those seen by the leader as not supportive or in compliance are labeled disloyal employees and are forced to live in what they perceive to be a hostile and oppressive organizational environment.

4. A *role culture* is often associated with large bureaucracies. In these organizational cultures personal power is often frowned on, expert power is tolerated, and position power is dominant.[11] Role culture organizations are highly structured, the employees are given clear, well-articulated objectives, goals, and procedures by their supervisor, and these employees are evaluated and rewarded on how well they meet these objectives and goals. However, role cultures can create an organization full of employees who simply follow the rules and don't know what happens outside their assigned area, which undermines creativity and causes change to develop slowly. As a result, the dysfunctional role culture–based organization stifles cooperation and collaboration among its employees and wastes the expertise of its employees.

It is important to remember that it is rare that organizations have one unified culture; rather, they have subcultures.[12] As a result, organizations have multiple dimensions of the four types of organizational cultures described above. This is why some groups or individuals within the same organization perceive and react to messages differently than other groups or individuals within the same organization. As a result there are several specific components of organizational cultures that can play a major role in efforts to lead change. These components do not individually define an organization's culture but are more indicative of the type of challenges one may encounter as part of the resistance to change. They focus on defining the relationship between the leaders of an organization who establish the overall direction of the organization, the middle managers who take the vision and directive forward and give it an operational framework, and the front-line staff and librarians who make it an embedded operational reality. Understanding these organizational culture models will provide insights into approaches one should use in communicating to different groups and individuals about the change initiative, which is discussed more in chapter 4.

CULTURE COMPONENTS THAT IMPACT CHANGE

The first component of an organizational culture that has a direct impact on successfully leading change is how much confidence each level of the organization has in the other. Since organizations rarely have one united culture but rather have multiple subcultures, the organization may have a "role culture" in one department while it has a "person culture" in another department. Unfortunately, the managers of the two departments may have little knowledge or understanding of "how things are done" in the other's department. Adding to this problem is the level of communication between these two departments. If there is a high level of communication with regular, respectful engagement, then the level of understanding of the job responsibilities between the employees and managers of the different departments is clearer. However, if there is a low level of communication, where little to no communication exists between units, then there is little understanding of the others' job responsibilities and little chance that employees have confidence or trust in each level of the organization, since they are more than likely unaware of how they will be impacted by the other department. There can even be different cultures within a single department, such as a task culture dominating for the more routine copy cataloging staff and their activities and a power culture of establishing standards to follow the national expectation for original cataloging librarians.

Another factor of organizations is whether there is trust or respect between the different cultures and layers of the organization. Trust has been a buzzword in management for some time, but is often misunderstood. Some would argue that trust and respect are the same or that one leads to the other. However, there is a difference between them and that true trust is actually quite rare, with most healthy organizations more likely having a good model for respect between the ranks. For many, trust represents a deeply personal relationship between individuals based on shared values and overall goodness of thought and action. According to Lucus, trust is the willingness of one party to be vulnerable to the actions of another party, and it is a function of access to information either through direct or indirect interactions.[13] Often you expect that someone you trust would never intentionally hurt you. If trust exists between two departments, it increases the chance of resource-sharing and knowledge transfer between the departments and reduces operational expenditures. The two departments will not feel it necessary to protect their own interests, and the knowledge transfer and resource-sharing can be absorbed and retained between the two departments. Basically, trust allows us to focus on the task at hand while knowing that those we trust are either protecting our interests or will not engage us in work-related activities that will be harmful to our unit.[14] This achievement will create an increase in the coordination of internal organizational processes, which leads to achieving internal excellence.[15]

In terms of leading change within libraries, trust can be a double-edged sword. On the one hand, one will not have to work as hard to gain buy-in from the top or communicate a concern from the front ranks because of a ready acceptance that everyone is working for the good of the organization without any personal agendas. One drawback of being in an organization with a high level of trust is that individuals are more likely to accept decisions or comments at face value and may actually be less likely to question the initiative in a constructive way. Having someone's trust can be its own burden because it can make a leader afraid to admit to making a mistake for fear of losing that trust. Similarly, trust once lost is extremely difficult to reestablish at an organizational culture level, particularly in libraries with low turnover where the past is clearly remembered by a persistent majority.

However, an organization that has respect between its ranks will have some characteristics of trust in believing that everyone is working toward the same primary goal but still have room for disagreement. Respect does not put people on a pedestal but leaves room for administrators or front-line staff to be human and own up to making mistakes. Similarly, it opens an environment where someone may be more comfortable questioning an idea because they know the person being questioned will be less likely to react in a defensive manner. Mutual respect helps support a professional environment while still allowing room for differences in beliefs. Finally, it is much harder to rebuild a culture that has been based on trust when something happens to destroy that trust. With the economic failures of the past several years, such as the Enron scandal, the mortgages crisis, and federal bailout packages, people are much less likely to trust, and trying to achieve this in connection with a change initiative can be setting the expectations for acceptance at unrealistic levels.

Another component of organization culture that can impact how change occurs is whether an organization's open communication models are based on merely acknowledging a person's comments and concerns or reaching to actually understand the comment or concern and thoughtfully respond to it. According to Armstrong, in order for organizations such as a library to achieve cultural change they need to "provide the opportunity for all levels of staff to become more involved in the organization's affairs; . . . [and] generate ideas from staff to develop the business, improve the levels of customer service and increase productivity."[16] Smith supports Armstrong's statement, stressing the importance of involving all the people who will carry out the changes in the change planning process.[17] Change will fail within the organization if it is imposed on staff by administration without real staff input. If change is to be effective and achieved, then a true partnership between administration and staff must be developed so that employees feel a true sense of challenge and continual commitment to the new change initiative. It is not uncommon for an organization that prides itself on having an open door or bottom-up feedback model to still fail when surveyed on communication. This is because at the top, administrators still apply an older management style that says that explaining a decision is the same as defending it, and defending a decision to lower-ranking staff is something that leaders should not do. They will welcome ideas that enhance their preconceived perceptions and priorities but only give minimal, superficial attention to ideas that ask them to think about an issue at a deeper level or challenge a decision they have already made.

In time with this model, individuals will quit making suggestions altogether because they know it is an exercise in futility.[18] This can lead to what Morrison and Milliken term organizational silence.[19] A clear indicator of this would be when a leader overhears employees talking and when encouraged by a peer to make a suggestion, the other employee responds with words like "Why bother?" or "No one listens to what I say" or "They will do what they want anyway." A similar signal would be to solicit feedback and not get much response, with little or none of it actually constructive or questioning. It is the authors' observations that individuals who work in contemporary libraries have inquiring minds and opinions about pretty much everything. Many scholars believe that for an organization to be successful and healthy, information (good or bad) must flow upward from the employees who do the practical work to those who are trying to administer a change initiative.[20] It is this upward flow of information that gives the administration divergent points of view that lead to effective organizational decision making. However, what is paradoxical is that even though there is a great deal of management rhetoric that focuses on empowerment and more open lines of communication, many employees in today's organizations report feeling that they cannot communicate up the chain of command about issues and problems.[21] The drawback is that leadership also loses good ideas that might have made an initiative even more successful. In the environment that seeks to understand a concern and thoughtfully respond to it, the contributor of the comment goes away having experienced a learning moment and having gained a better understanding of why one's suggestion was not adopted. While this is a more time-consuming approach and generally requires leaders to check their egos at the door, it will position an organization much more effectively for future change initiatives. In essence this is the classic difference between hearing and active listening, and it is a key component of servant leadership. Consequently some scholars argue that true empowerment is rare and is not the norm in most organizations.[22] The situational aspects of empowerment and establishing realistic expectations are discussed more in chapter 5.

Another factor of organizational culture that can play into how change initiatives are managed is an understanding of the political power structure. Is the power—that is, decision making—centralized with a core group of administrators or middle managers? Or is it distributed throughout the organization in a structured manner where all employees have a clear understanding of their own sphere of decision-making influence? Leaders may have to adapt their communication and planning activities within the context of the model favored by the organizational culture. One can still get value-added input and operational decision-making buy-in from the front-line staff in a centralized power model, but it may be necessary to more clearly explain what is expected from front-line staff and help them develop decision-making skills. A related factor to this cultural area is whether an organization is transparent in its decision making or instead appears to have a high element of hypocrisy where decision-making words and actions do not agree. An organization that claims to have decentralized decision making but starts every meeting with the leaders stating their opinion of what should be happening or what a model should look like before asking for the opinions of others is not transparent. Instead the leaders will come across as hypocritical in having intentionally squelched ideas, especially when combined with a style of listening that acknowledges but does not engage in dialogue on comments. This is a particularly serious issue when dealing with Generation X and Millennials in middle management or leadership-potential positions, as they have an extremely low tolerance for hypocrisy, equating it with injustice.[23] A related issue can come up when doing work-space changes if employees have been accustomed to have decision-making authority or perceived ownership in relation to their desk furniture configurations, chairs, desktop workstations, or square footage, but then are overridden by institutional mandates.

There is one final aspect of organization culture that can determine where a change initiative will have to be reinforced by the change leader to keep it from faltering: whether an organization's culture is focused on the past or the future. In the former, organizational memory is revered and a frequent response to any proposed change is "We already tried that and it did not work." In this environment, a change leader is going to have to work more at putting changes in context so that even as a particular change process is being revisited, experienced staff can more easily understand that the environmental factors are different enough to warrant giving the idea another try. Most organizational theorists believe that "an organization's major emphasis must be on the future and providing continuous value for external customers and stakeholders."[24] A good explanation can be to suggest that part of the reason it was not successful in the past was that it was ahead of its time. For an organization that has a robust, future-oriented culture, a change leader may need to actually slow staff members down to encourage them to fully think through an initiative to head off repeating mistakes of the past. It may also be difficult for people with this cultural mindset to recognize when they have run up against the need to limit the plan or implement it in a prototype model. This could be due to budget constraints or support timelines, such as the amount of staff available to do construction projects or the need to get approval paperwork to establish a new position. Leading through delays is presented in more depth in chapter 6.

CHANGING A LIBRARY'S ORGANIZATIONAL CULTURE ⎯

All organizations, including libraries, have deep-rooted values that may run counter to the changing environment. Consequently, these values that support the foundations of their existing culture become inappropriate and at times detrimental to the needs of patrons. Beugelsdijk, Koen, and Noorderhaven believe that this type of negative influence creates a feeling of "we-ness."[25] Once the members of an organization discover this they begin the attempt to change their organizational culture. However, Schien believes that the first step toward changing an organizational culture is to understand what the current organizational structure is and then decide what needs to change.[26] If an administration begins implementing a change without understanding the current organizational culture, then they may be faced with unforeseen and potentially negative consequences. Schien also believes that a manager must understand the mechanisms used to move an organizational culture and how assumptions about the values that make up the culture are interpreted and communicated to employees.[27] He states that once these mechanisms are discovered, a manager can then outline the foundation of a plan to change the organization's culture.[28]

It is possible to change an organizational culture at the same time that one is leading an operational change initiative. However, this is not easy or quick or even advised. When changing organizational culture, one has to exercise patience and measure progress in small increments. One also has to be prepared for the dance-step effect of gaining and losing ground, such as the cliché of "two steps forward, one step back." One aspect of changing organizational culture is demonstrating clear commitment through words *and* actions of the culture you are trying to foster. Leadership by example can be instrumental in demonstrating commitment to a cultural change.[29] At times the lines between the organizational culture change and the actual operational change initiative can get blurred, and it can be difficult to stay focused and on track with each. It is important not to base the success of the operational change on the ability to totally turn around the organizational culture. This is because the momentum behind an organizational culture is much greater. Just as it is more difficult to turn a fully loaded book truck than a lightly loaded one, it will be easier to implement smaller changes within a slowly changing organizational cultural framework. This means that your operational change techniques will need to be constantly adapting to the current state of the organizational culture.

For example, suppose you set out to change the organizational culture power model so that employees have more decision-making authority in implementing changes. If the past culture has been one of highly directive, centralized power where employees were told what to do in detail by an authority figure, then they probably will not have the decision-making skills to take on basic decision making with regard to their own workflow. During the first operational change, one may have to guide the employees into simple decision making by the use of leading questions. "What do you think we should do?" and "Why do you think we should do (blank)?" become your most frequently asked questions. At this point, you cannot charge them to go off and implement a change because you would be setting them up to fail. Fast-forward three years: now you can charge a team to bring back answers to key functions in an operational change, but you will still need to define the charge rather narrowly. Fast-forward another three years and one can now set an overall operational initiative and let a team create the framework and decide how to make it work. The purpose of this example is to illustrate that changing culture is a progressive process that may take the experience of accomplishing several successful change initiatives for staff to build their confidence and comfort in developing innovative processes and procedures.

ANTICIPATING CULTURE PROBLEMS

The previous sections have detailed where organizational culture can intersect with change initiatives. Since changing organizational culture will not happen overnight, it becomes extremely important to recognize what problems in implementing change might be tied to the organizational culture. Do you need to overcome a trust issue as you communicate the reasons for the change? Will you need to take time to engage with individuals to allay concerns? Are you suggesting something that was tried in the past and failed? Are you suggesting something that was tried in the past and was successful but staff had been convinced to let go of it? In this last scenario, the key is to avoid loss of leadership credibility when naysayers relish making "I told you so" statements. Are you suggesting staff or librarians take on a task that has been associated with a different employee classification, such as technical support? Will there be a perception that the work is more or less "professional"? Are you going to need to put the brakes on enthusiasm in order to deal with budget constraints?

By doing an organizational culture scan for a project, you can better anticipate and incorporate the time needed to address cultural issues in your planning and implementation timeline. Just as you must factor in a training window for staff to develop new skills, you may need to factor in time for them to adjust their overall way of thinking about the organization. This can be particularly critical if you are bringing together different organizational cultures as part of a departmental reorganization. Suppose you decided to merge the serials back-room processes of acquisitions and cataloging with the storefront processes of helping users in a serials collection. You may be mixing two or three significantly different organizational cultures. Without stopping to provide some "getting to know you" and acclimation time, the cultural clash will serve to undermine a lot of progress in making any successful operational or integrated workflow changes. The merger will actually become competitive between the units as each tries to sustain its organizational culture.

MANAGERIAL DISCONNECTS

The fact that you are reading this book is an indicator that you want to improve your skills as a leader or manager. Unfortunately, this is not the same for all of your peers.

People find themselves in managerial or leadership roles for a variety of reasons. In some cases, they will have sought out the opportunity for professional growth and development. In other cases, the role will have found them because an administrator thought they had the skills needed to lead an initiative or department. Regardless of why one has found oneself in a leadership role, one will bring the framework of one's own organizational experience to the table.

Individual managers will view the presence and value of organizational culture in different ways. This can lead to disconnects with your peers as you engage on organizational culture issues when you lead a particular change initiative. The key is to recognize where your own limitations or biases are in what you can impact in the library-wide organizational culture. You may not be able to change how an administrator views the decision-making process or a peer manager's tendency to acknowledge and dismiss a comment or concern instead of seeking to understand the source of it, but you can work to establish a local organizational culture on the particular team you are leading or department that you manage.

By the same token, there may be peer managers who have engaged in effective change leadership and effective management of organizational culture. These are managers that you should look at emulating, and you should study the approaches they used. Seek to understand a cause-and-effect relationship with cultural overtones to explore how others have been successful in leading changes.

KEYS TO SUCCESS

In pulling together the information in this chapter, one can develop a series of statements to try and follow as a successful leader of change when dealing with organizational culture.

- Recognize that organizational culture affects change and change affects organizational culture.
- Try to understand the organizational culture of the stakeholders before trying to make changes.
- Realize that there are subcultures within an organization and these subcultures may vary over time, functions, and staff composition, so broad assumptions about the organization's culture will not be valid.
- Remember that communication is a two-way street that requires engaged listening and speaking for all participants in the conversation.

- Recognize that a change which requires a significant organizational culture shift for success will be more difficult to carry forward and will take longer to accomplish.

THINKING EXERCISES

1. How would you describe the organizational culture in your immediate unit? The library as a whole?

2. Can you think about how different leaders and individuals seem to resonate better with different organizational culture models?

3. Identify one element of the organizational culture in your department that you would like to see modified. How might you go about initiating this cultural change? (Note: Be sure and choose something small to start with.)

4. What are the biggest challenges you would face in getting buy-in and sustaining the cultural change you identified in exercise 3?

NOTES

1. M. Jason Martin, "That's the Way We Do Things Around Here: An Overview of Organizational Culture," *Electronic Journal of Academic and Special Librarianship* 7 (Spring 2006), http://southernlibrarianship.icaap.org/content/v07n01/martin_m01.htm.
2. Edgar Schein, "Organizational Culture and Leadership," in *Classics of Organization Theory*, ed. Jay Shafritz and J. Steven Ott (Fort Worth: Harcourt College, 2001), 373–74.
3. Terrence E. Deal and Allan A. Kennedy, *Corporate Cultures: The Rites and Rituals of Corporate Life* (Reading, MA: Addison-Wesley, 1982).
4. Ann T. Jordan, *Business Anthropology* (Prospect Heights, IL: Waveland, 2003), 85.
5. Deal and Kennedy, *Corporate Cultures*.
6. Martin "That's the Way We Do Things Around Here."
7. Deal and Kennedy, *Corporate Cultures*.
8. Gareth Morgan, *Images of Organization* (Beverly Hills, CA: Sage, 1986).
9. Charles B. Handy, *Understanding Organisations* (Harmondsworth, UK: Penguin Books, 1985).
10. Ibid.
11. Ibid.
12. Peter B. Smith and Mark F. Peterson, *Leadership, Organizations and Culture* (London: Sage, 1988).

13. Leyland M. Lucus, "The Impact of Trust and Reputation on the Transfer of Best Practices," *Journal of Knowledge Management* 9, no. 4 (2005): 87–101.
14. Ibid.
15. Dimitris Folinas and others, "E-volution of a Supply Chain: Cases and Best Practices," *Internet Research* 14, no. 4 (2004): 274–83.
16. Michael Armstrong, *A Handbook of Personnel Management Practice*, 4th ed. (London: Kogan Page, 1991).
17. Ian Smith, "Continuing Professional Development and Workplace Learning: Achieving Successful Organizational Change—Do's and Don'ts of Change Management," *Library Management* 27, no. 4/5 (2006): 300–306.
18. Ibid.
19. Elizabeth Wolfe Morrison and Frances J. Milliken, "Organizational Silence: A Barrier to Change and Development in a Pluralistic World," *Academy of Management Review* 25 (October 2000): 706–25.
20. William Edwards Deming, *Out of the Crisis* (Cambridge, MA: MIT Press, 1986); David M. Saunders and others, "Employee Voice to Supervisors," *Employee Responsibilities and Rights Journal* 5 (September 1992): 241–59.
21. Jeffrey Pfeffer, *Competitive Advantage through People* (Boston: Harvard Business School Press, 1994); Gretchen Spreitzer, "Psychological Empowerment in the Workplace: Dimensions, Measurement, and Validation," *Academy of Management Journal* 38, no. 5 (1995): 1442–65; Morrison and Milliken, "Organizational Silence."
22. Joseph H. Foegen, "Why Not Empowerment?" *Business and Economic Review* 45 (April–June 1999): 31–33.
23. Pixey Anne Mosley, "Mentoring Gen X Managers: Tomorrow's Library Leadership Is Already Here," *Library Administration & Management* 19, no. 4 (Fall 2005): 185–92.
24. Amos Lakos and Shelley Phipps, "Creating a Culture of Assessment: A Catalyst for Organizational Change," *Portal: Libraries and the Academy* 4, no. 3 (2004): 345–61.
25. Sjoerd Beugelsdijk, Carla Koen, and Niels Noorderhaven, "A Dyadic Approach to the Impact of Differences in Organizational Culture on Relationship Performance," *Industrial Marketing Management* 38 (2009): 312–23.
26. Edgar Schien, *Organizational Culture and Leadership* (San Francisco: Jossey-Bass 1985).
27. Ibid.
28. Ibid.
29. Lakos and Phipps, "Creating a Culture of Assessment."

INITIATING CHANGE EFFECTIVELY

Good communication does not mean that you have
to speak in perfectly formed sentences and paragraphs.
It isn't about slickness. Simple and clear go a long way.

—John Kotter

THE PAST SEVERAL chapters have focused on understanding the role of change in an organization and understanding the emotions and reactions that people have to change. This knowledge helps one lead others through the change process in a way that optimizes buy-in to the change and is responsive to concerns. So having read this, you are ready to implement the change, right? Wrong. Implementation is actually a small part of the entire process of leading change. The first part of actively and effectively leading change is to initially sell the idea to all of the stakeholders—and how the manager sells the idea depends on what is changing. Announcing that the library is changing the location of its new bookshelf is different than announcing that the library is going to relocate and merge the reference desk with the circulation desk. Simply sharing the idea and explaining it is not enough. Managers need to remember that long-term and embedded change doesn't happen successfully simply because a library administrator wants it to happen. Change can be successful only if it is effectively managed, and the first step is to understand the extent to which the change alters the status quo.[1] As the magnitude of change increases, employees view the communication coming from managers about the change in an increasingly negative light because their sense of security is increasingly threatened. Due to this reason, managers need to communicate the explanation for the change in a more inductive and elaborate way.

Adding to this problem, managers sometimes consider change to be a separate entity with a clear definable framework, as if nothing went before and nothing comes after, frozen in time and space.[2] These latter assumptions have been the downfall of many organizational changes projects since they do not take into consideration the emotional content of the change within the context of the mood of the organization. In 2006 a survey suggested that only 6 percent of change management projects were completely successfully (with a further 32 percent "mostly" successful) because the mood of the organization during the time of change was not considered. According to Green, the survey showed that during the changes the mood of the organization directly affected the outcome of the change projects. (See table below.)[3]

MOOD EXPRESSED ABOUT CHANGE	SUCCESSFUL PROJECTS (%)	UNSUCCESSFUL PROJECTS (%)
Anxiety	44	51
Confusion	22	43
Frustration	23	44
Fatigue	24	34
Resistance	24	28

Confident leaders may do everything right in that they follow what is going on in the community of professional peers (the American Library Association, Association of Research Libraries, or "other libraries like us") and understand the administrative motivations behind the change decisions. Yet when the leader tries to explain the purpose and build buy-in, the entire program flounders as others do not buy into the change. This is why organizational change leaders recognize that although it is important to communicate change clearly and in different venues to their employees, it is still difficult to build the connection between what they are saying and what actually gets done.[4] This lack of connection between what is communicated and what is done is because the typical employee does not think like a leader does and both view change differently.[5] Most employees are connected more with what they do in their job rather than the purpose of the job. Strebel calls this connection "personal compact." According to Strebel, employees and organizations have shared obligations and commitments that define their working relationship, and any change initiatives alter these obligations and commitments.[6]

Even librarians who are active in professional associations tend to focus on their immediate, expert service areas and do not tend to actively engage in the "future of the library" discussions where the entire role of reference, cataloging, or reserve services are questioned. In truth, there is an even more serious flaw in the previous perspective because when it comes to change initiatives, there is no such thing as a typical employee. Everyone's personal idiosyncrasies, assumptions, and biases come to the forefront as one deals with change, and the effective leader must speak to these different listening skills, learning styles, and personal filters to build buy-in for a change before one ever starts the actual implementation process. As discussed in earlier chapters, despite the fact that organizational change is frequently about change in structures, hierarchy, or technology, it is achieved through the individual. Organizational change will fail if change leaders underestimate the importance of the individual.[7]

COMMON COMMUNICATION MISTAKES

Communication is considered to be a critical factor in implementing change within an organization because effective communication is the tool that introduces, explains, and prepares employees for the upcoming change. If managers communicate change effectively to their employees, they can help to increase employee understanding of the administrative commitment to change as well as reduce confusion and resistance to it.[8] If managers possess poor communication skills, then this will be a major barrier to implementing change. Managers with excellent communication skills who build enthusiastic buy-in will have a greater pattern of leading successful change. Some leaders may have a different set of challenges, such as keeping overenthusiastic staff grounded to implementation realities without undermining their positive approach.

The first part of initiating communication about change is to effectively explain to the people involved why the change is needed, and to do this the change manager needs to have a clear "vision of direction or goals of the change in order to know where they need to go."[9] Many leaders or managers are accused of making changes to fix something that is not broken or a problem that does not exist. This is a normal response that should be the first cue for leaders to realize that they have not effectively explained the reason for the change to build buy-in and have already put the change initiative at risk of floundering. According to Lewis, change managers must provide their employees with a consistent and compelling explanation for the need to change.[10] There are several reasons why this is one of the hardest parts of getting a change going. The first is that employees are comfortable with the status quo and often identify with their jobs and invest in them at a personal level.[11] When one starts saying there is a problem, many employees interpret that remark with a filter to mean they are not doing their job well or they are part of the problem. Similarly, saying a service is no longer needed because user expectations have changed can come across as "you" are no longer of value to library users and are not needed, which increases distrust in the organization and destroys the relationship between employees and their superiors.[12] Instead of simply announcing that interlibrary service response times are too long and are a problem, and thereby immediately alienating all of the staff responsible for the area, one should comment on a need to look at the processes and workflows to see if the library can streamline operations for improved efficiencies to meet the new consortia expectations. It is critical for leaders to use language that depersonalizes the problem and focuses on the process or the environment, rather than the job being done by an individual.

Another hurdle leaders face is that the ability to anticipate, understand, and predict large-scale trends is not usually highly developed among front-line staff. What may seem to be a perfectly intuitive, cause-and-effect relationship to a leader may be less apparent to someone immersed in the daily activities of running the library. One example of this that libraries have struggled with in the past is in relating initiatives to a growing desire on the users' part for more independence or self-reliance. Obviously, the staff members sitting at a service desk do not see this broad trend because some people are still coming to them for assistance. They do not necessarily see that they are helping only a small part of the user community, who may in fact represent the underachievers. They can find it difficult to "see" the self-reliant students earning "A" and "B" grades on the assignment who are directly accessing online resources. It is more difficult for one immersed in a process to see patterns in usage that may be more obvious from an administrative perspective.

An organizational history of trust in the administrators will carry a message up to a point, but the more drastic the change the more skepticism a leader will encounter in taking it forward. In organizations where administrative trust has not been established or has been damaged in the past, it becomes even more critical to communicate and build agreement on the need for a change to occur. According to Shel Holtz, one of the main reasons why change is resisted is due to lack of trust.[13] Employees may simply not trust the change manager or library administration, and as a result employees will suspect the motivation behind the decision to change. For example, how often are employees told by their change manager that before change occurs everyone will be trained on the new change, and the change occurs more rapidly than expected and no training is done by the change manager? Or the training is perceived as inadequate or insensitive to different learning style needs. As a result, resistance to change becomes inevitable. Exploring the need for the change can actually be difficult for some managers and leaders for several reasons. At a personal and emotional level, many managers or administrators resent this activity because it feels like they are being required to explain or justify a decision. Similarly, if employees question the validity of the statements being used as a justification, the manager or administrator tends to respond defensively, as if to a personal attack on their credibility. At this point, rather than providing clarification and improving buy-in, the communication breaks down and often ends with the leader eventually responding as in a cartoon, "I'm the boss and I say do it." As a result, employees might react to this managerial defensive reaction by not responding at all, even when asked for input by the manager. Scholars believe that employees in "many organizations know the truth about certain issues and problems within the organization yet dare not speak the truth to their superiors."[14] The reason for this is that many organizations are by and large intolerant of opposition, and because of this employees are less likely to speak out about problems and challenge beliefs for fear of negative repercussions.[15] This silence can create a significant barrier to achieving organizational success during change initiatives.[16]

Communication problems can also come from "expertise" overload. Like the distinguished mathematics professor trying to teach basic calculus, it can be extremely difficult for the experienced administrator or manager to back away from the big picture and be able to effectively engage with a librarian or staff member on the front lines to explain the need for organizational changes in a way that explains how their roles and responsibilities will be changed. This is particularly problematic for administrators or managers who have immersed themselves in positioning the library for the future. The other aspect of this distance problem is that the visionary manager or administrator, who has focused on developing the big picture or strategic position of the department, may no longer have an accurate picture of what is currently happening in the unit from a detailed operational perspective. Making a statement or comment that connects the new initiative to an obsolete procedure seriously damages the leader's credibility as a change leader and will affect the success of the communication effort.[17] This is where leaders must be careful in how an idea is communicated and work with supervisors and operational leaders on connecting the vision to the operational level.

One huge mistake that every manager or leader will make at some point in their career is to announce the problem and the organization's solution to the problem in the same meeting, discussion, or e-mail. This happens for a number of reasons. In some cases the initiative has already been developed at an administrative or even institutional level, and by the time it reaches the middle manager or team leader for implementation, it is fairly well defined and non-negotiable. In other cases, a manager or leadership team will have explored a problem and developed a solution by working from the big picture, and that solution is then announced as an implementation. There are several reasons this approach sets one up to experience problems in moving a change forward. First, it is too much information for many individuals to fully comprehend at one time. Second, it prompts too much of a shock reaction or trauma-based approach. If you have not previously laid out the problem or announced the issue was being explored, it leaves employees responding in an emotional model with rational thinking suspended. Finally, it sends a subliminal message where people feel marginalized in not having had an opportunity to participate and lend their expertise or experience to the search for a solution. According to Lewis, participation in implementing change furnishes employees with a sense of control over the change and decreases their feelings of doubt about how the change will affect them directly; they will therefore be more committed to the change and less opposed to its goals and objectives.[18] Just announcing the solution to a problem also sends a message to the employees of leadership arrogance through not having engaged with employees in developing the solution. The net result is that it leaves employees feeling that their buy-in and expertise are not important and that their opinion is irrelevant, often leading employees to participate in the organizational silence mentioned in previous chapters.

One final caution to consider is when communicating about potential changes to front-line staff. Many managers feel that front-line staff members are typically not interested in high-level considerations at an institutional level until the details have been sorted out. For this reason, they will filter updates and the information they are sharing with their staff. However, in doing so, they set their staff up to be surprised when a change is actually implemented and left feeling they were excluded from previous discussions. Ultimately, a pattern of this will erode staff trust in the managers and administrators. For this reason, it is important for managers to anticipate the potential impact of institutional dialogues and share these as possible future changes that lack clear definition. An example of this might be an institution deciding to include support of diversity initiatives as an expectation in everyone's position description, with associated goals that will be evaluated. If a manager has not passed along that the institution is exploring the issue and provided some explanation or context for the change, then the individual is left wondering where something came from when it is enacted perceptually out of the blue with the weight of law.

COMMUNICATING THE NEED THROUGH THE USE OF A CLEAR VISION

One of the key parts of initiating change is that leaders must verify and persuasively communicate to all stakeholders the reason why the change is needed. One way to convince individuals of the need for change is to craft a vision that offers the hope of relief from stress or discomfort.[19] The main point that change leaders need to remember is that they must communicate change clearly in order to build support among their employees for successful change and reduce resistance. It is important for change leaders to remember that change involves a political process where they must grow and cultivate widespread support and participation by organizational members in order to overcome resistance to change.[20]

When communicating the reason behind the change, it is important to recognize that individuals will be hearing the information through their own filters, and it is critical to approach the issues in ways that allow for different learning styles. Some library employees will be engaged verbal listeners who are systematic thinkers and can immediately grasp the implications of the need for the change and begin brainstorming and analyzing possible solutions. However, other employees may be initially nonresponsive and need a chance to take the information away and process it more thoughtfully. They may need an opportunity to come back to the table and ask clarifying questions before they can engage in developing solutions. Finally, another group may disagree with the identified need for the change. The traditional approach in dealing with these employees is to ignore or marginalize this latter group while working most closely with those that are immediately on board.

However, this shortsighted approach will often have a high price further down the road. While the change may get off the ground quicker, it will grind to a halt when it reaches the actual implementation stages. In other words, the irresistible force will meet the immovable object and often the immovable object will win in the end. For change to be truly successful, it is necessary to actively engage with the resistant employees and at least bring them to a neutral position of accepting, tolerating, and participating in the change, even if they cannot bring themselves to fully cheer it on. This necessity is part of what sets libraries, particularly public institutions, truly apart from the corporate world. Whether it is tenured librarians or the library assistants with twenty years of longevity who have bought into the lower pay/higher stability of the state or civil service employee model, libraries in public institutions often have less flexibility in turning over staff for the convenience of administrative change initiatives.

Rather than waiting for the change to get up a head of steam in the hopes it will bowl over the naysayers, a more effective approach to leading change is to work on engagement by all from the initial stages. This requires that one spend more time presenting the background information behind a change initiative in different ways. It means one has to engage one-on-one or through managerial agents to build a true understanding of "why" one has reached particular positions.[21] It may be necessary to ask dissenters to consider new ideas rather than demand they adopt your own reasoning. It also means that one needs to go back to chapter 3 and try to understand why the dissenter does not understand the reason for the change. Is it a philosophical or value-based perspective? Are you assuming individuals have knowledge they do not really have?

MAKING IT RELEVANT

One key element in preparing someone for a change is to explain the rationale behind the change in such a way that the listeners can realize the potential impact on them. Simply giving an update or mentioning a trend is not enough to automatically create buy-in. An effective change leader will provide context and even a slight sense of urgency that encourages those employees one is leading to connect cause-and-effect or stakeholder impact to more abstract issues.[22] Similarly, change leaders can help establish a tone that prepares employees for change by discussing the potential impact even as the actual details of a change have not been worked out. Another way of making it relevant is when the actual changes taking place are in a different unit, but there is the potential for indirect impact in the manager's unit. For example, suppose a reference department is going through a major organizational change with a new service model and new resource priorities. On the surface, this would not appear to have an impact on cataloging or acquisitions staff. However, it has an underlying impact on the emotional resilience of the reference staff, which can translate to being short-tempered or tending to overreact to problems with the catalog or in placing new book orders, thereby increasing the tension and potential for conflict between the departments. In this case, it is important for the cataloging and acquisitions department staff to be made aware that another department is going through a stressful period of change. Similarly, providing updates of library-level initiatives, such as the acquisition of a large special collection, can be related to what it might mean: increased questions for reference staff and different records to process for cataloging staff. The results of a new user study may mean that new administrative priorities or performance goals could be established.

Unfortunately, unless the leader is fairly explicit, employees at the time may not realize what the leader is doing. Typical of any organization, there are ambivalent, self-oriented employees in libraries who prefer the approach of "Just tell me when it is real" or "I only want to know what has been decided." These individuals see the testing of ideas with brainstorming, verbal discussion, or even prototyping as a waste of time, particularly if an idea does not prove as feasible as initially expected. An effective change leader must find an approach to help these employees realize that there is a difference between hearing irrelevant reports and relevant updates that prepare one for change.[23]

KEEPING IT SIMPLE

Another aspect of communicating the purpose and background for an impending change is to put it into terms that people can understand. This can be difficult when a department is larger and has a wide range of experiences and perspectives represented by its staff. If managers are looking at one of the more experienced staff members while talking rather than at a newer individual, they may not realize someone is confused. It can be easy for an experienced manager to report about budgets and fiscal year closure, circulation policies, virtual reference, MARC updates, and so on and never realize how much of what one says is in jargon that leaves newer staff in the dark.[24] Similarly, one cannot automatically assume that even experienced staff members have a deeper comprehension of library-wide practices outside of one's immediate area. Some individuals, particularly those who are less effective at auditory learning and gain understanding based on context, may sit through meeting after meeting without understanding a significant part of what is being said. One way to address this is to encourage staff members who may have missed something to follow up with you or their immediate supervisor. One can also frequently call for any questions about an update. Then when someone is brave enough to ask for basic clarification, praise them for having brought up something others may be wondering about as well. When doing this, it is absolutely essential that one maintains supportive body language and control in one's comments. Coming across as phony in repeatedly saying, "What a good question that is" or letting go of the long-suffering sigh or sarcastic "again" when someone asks you to explain something that you have covered in the past, will kill openness to speaking up to learn more. Similarly, even while one is trying to avoid too much jargon, it is also important to avoid coming across as talking down to experienced staff. Finding the balance is a challenge and will vary depending on the individual departmental composition. If there is a wide disparity in experience, it may even be appropriate to meet with smaller subgroups of employees that have similar levels of experience rather than risk disengagement or confused understanding.

ESTABLISHING THE FRAMEWORK FOR BUY-IN ————

There are several other challenges in effectively communicating the reason for a change and what level of input front-line library staff should expect to have. In some cases, the change will be a department-level operational or process issue where the staff members that do the task have a direct say in the new process. Other changes will be at a larger level in the library and involve several departments. In this scenario, the department heads or designated representatives may have an opportunity to bring feedback to a planning group, but all members of a department will not have a direct say in the development of the change. One particular challenge for managers is when another department is going through a significant change and the peripheral impact of that change on their own department is overlooked. In this situation, the stakeholders are usually defined as those that are directly impacted. In these cases, it is the responsibility of the peripheral department head to stay engaged in dialogues so that when a peer manager or administrator mentions an initiative with impact, the department head should bring it to the community's attention. Additionally, there may be some changes where an administrative or managerial decision has to be made because it will not be possible to reach a satisfactory consensus or majority decision from the front-line staff members. This can be unfeasible because of the scope of knowledge needed behind the decision and lack of opportunity to learn on the part of the front-line staff. It can also be that it requires a particularly strong training in thinking of the library as a more abstract system than at the detailed operations level. This is frequently the model used in developing the annual budget and making broad decisions on developing and launching new services.

Another aspect of establishing input expectations on the part of staff has to do with how conflicting input will be handled and whether the input is perceived as binding on administrators. This latter area is one that contributes to massive confusion and often develops into a trust issue, or rather an issue of betrayed trust when administrators take action in opposition to the front-line recommendations. The key is to build into the model recognition that even as input is being sought, there may be some immutable points that are not subject to bottom-up revision. Usually, the non-negotiable items address establishing the main direction the library is going. For example, suppose a library decides to bring in a coffee shop. Many traditional-minded staff and librarians will probably oppose the idea. In this situation, a leader cannot ask for their input or give an implicit promise to follow it because the input will be contrary to the overarching plan. However, once the base framework—putting in a coffee shop—is established, input can be credibly sought for detailed aspects of the implementation, such as what type of flooring should be used in the vicinity, will users be allowed to take the coffee anywhere or need to stay in the vicinity, and even what to name it. The other aspect of soliciting input is that it requires the leader to be willing to bend and give up control of every detail because in all likelihood what the front-line staff comes up with will not be what the leader or manager would have chosen.

Unfortunately, on some occasions institutional events will move at such a fast pace that there will not be time to lay out the details of an issue and go through the process of soliciting input. Some examples of this are when there is an unexpected budget shortfall or windfall late in a fiscal year. In this case, it may be necessary for the library leadership to step into the decision-maker role and analyze the situation and take action in a very short timeline. If leaders find themselves in this position, follow-up communication as soon as possible is critical. They should send e-mails letting employees know what is transpiring. Normally this would not be the optimal way to communicate with the group, but even less effective communication is better than no communication at all, with the rumor mill running rampant over snippets someone has read about in the local newspaper, overheard in passing, or picked up from a copy machine or networked printer observation. In this situation, the role of the leader is to send a message that gives confidence that one is acting on the situation thoughtfully and seeking advice as appropriate given the short timeline and nature of the event. Once decisions have been reached, they should be communicated as soon as possible. Rather than explain why one made a particular decision in a defensive way, leaders should focus on helping others to follow their rationale in coming to the conclusion they did and open the door for feedback that might contribute to a different conclusion in the future.

EMPOWERING OTHERS

Even during the early stages of initiating change, empowerment can be a factor to help the change to be successful as it is implemented. At this stage, one is utilizing empowerment to build a support base for the project. It is an aspect of peer pressure, used in a positive and encouraging way. Librarians and staff members who see their peers recognizing the positive potential for a change initiative will be more likely to listen with an open mind, or at least with less cynical skepticism.[25] This is particularly true if the peer is an individual for whom they have a lot of respect or perceive to be a grassroots leader.[26] As such it is important for the leaders of the change to identify the unofficial leaders among the staff and engage with them as part of the change initiation process, in addition to working through the traditional organizational hierarchy.

This engagement must be done in a deliberatively casual manner, which may sound like an oxymoron to those with a direct leadership style. It is important that the person be engaged in conversation about the pending change activities at a level that makes it a two-way conversation. This means setting the stage carefully. Rather than asking employees to leave their comfort zone by coming to the manager's office, the manager should drop by the employees' work space. If this is not possible because of an open-office architectural layout in the staff area and it is necessary to meet in the manager's office, schedule the appointment in a way that is inviting and does not prompt the employee to announce to peers, "Uh-oh, I'm being called to the boss's office" in the voice of doom or in a tone of "I'm in trouble." One can set it up with a subject line of "Seeking your input" or "Needing your opinion."

Once the employee arrives, use visitor seating to put both of you on a conversational footing that avoids the hierarchical symbolism of talking across the desk. Offer basic hospitality amenities, such as bottled water or other beverages and finger toys for those who tend to think best with their hands engaged. Then outline in bare bones the change one is thinking of implementing and the basic justification for it. Closely watch and use active listening when gauging the response by the employee. In this way a leader learns what issues may come up as the idea is announced broadly and have responses prepared in anticipation of the questions. At this point, one may want to engage in dialogue to build a better understanding of the employee's thoughts and answer questions to help the individual understand your perspective as the leader. It is important not to become too defensive to concerns that the individual raises; otherwise, it appears that it is more than a considered idea but rather one that has already been decided. Similarly, it is important not to encourage the employee to jump to recommending specific implementation models. One can brainstorm different approaches to use, but speak carefully to avoid the impression that one is committing in the course of the meeting to a particular approach. For example, suppose one was looking at relocating a unit to a different part of the library. You might discuss with the employee what the best or worst times of the year are, in terms of workload. Or you might discuss whether there are any lingering issues from the current configuration that the move gives the organization an opportunity to address, such as an ineffective mail sorter or inadequate space for support tools or supplies that employees need regular access to.

Finally, thank the employee for taking the time away from one's responsibilities to meet with you. It is important at this point not to put a gag order on the employee because in doing so, you undermine the grassroots leadership role. Instead, let the person know that you will think about what has been said and will take it into consideration as you develop your plans. The manager should encourage the employee to follow up with an e-mail or another appointment if additional ideas come to mind. When discussing the issues from the meeting with other employees, ask the employee to present it as a "possibility." This approach will plant seeds for support and buy-in later. The important thing is to project sincerity and appreciation for the individual's contributions. The last thing a manager wants is grassroots leaders leaving meetings feeling they have been manipulated or strong-armed to agree with a forthcoming announcement. Even if the plan undergoes a significant shift based on what one ends up considering the best solution, one will have used the informal employee peer network to prepare employees that a change may be coming and even give them a sense of what the change might be, with the operative word being "might." This also sends a message that one is seeking input and engagement and empowering others to be a part of the change.

RECOGNIZING HOW STAFF ARE RESPONDING

As one has initiated the communication about a change, it is important to do a periodic pulse check to verify how people are responding and assess this response in the context of earlier chapters on understanding change resistance. In doing so, it is important to be careful as one seeks out this information and puts it in a perspective that takes into consideration the scale of the change, the individuals involved, the level of stability or instability of decision making about the change, and the passage of time since the change announcement.

First, decide what you need to learn and look for signs among your staff. It does not do any good to know that a particular department is not happy about a proposed change. This is too broad and nonspecific. What you need to know is *why* they are not happy. What is it about the change that is making them unhappy? Are they concerned about losing something? Do they feel disenfranchised? Is there historical baggage that has become problematic? Is it something specific that can be easily addressed, such as a desk configuration or schedule adjustment issue? Or is it something that is overarching to the entire project, such as a philosophical disagreement with the direction? Also, how unhappy are they? Is it at the nervous grumbling over being inconvenienced stage, or the worrying about an ambiguous future stage? Or is it at the heels-dug-in, near revolt stage? Admittedly all of these questions imply a predisposal toward a negative reaction, and it is possible for classified staff and librarians to be positively engaged about the pending change from the start and throughout the process. However, this is not the norm, since we recognize that change is difficult for many people and is not automatically perceived as a desired event even though the ultimate result will be a positive one. Even when one is engaged in a positive change experience, such as replacing worn-out office or public furniture, there will be concerns and opinions from a wide variety of perspectives about disruptions, lost work time, or appropriate use of funds. In leading all changes, the old adage about "only being able to please some of the people some of the time" comes into play. However, it is important that a leader does not fall back on this as an excuse for not continuing to communicate and engage with employees to encourage them to support the change.

Next, decide how you get the information. If you have established lines of communication with employees where they feel comfortable speaking up, then this means getting out and talking to them. If there is a culture of distrust that inhibits others from speaking up, it may mean one has to fall back on sending out anonymous surveys or bringing in neutral mediators to ask about concerns. Next decide who you want to ask to get this information. This does not mean letting managers gloss over that "everything is fine" because they do not want their units to appear to cause problems or be perceived that they are not doing their job as managers. It also does not mean you want to go directly to the employee who is known to have the highest level of resistance to any proposed change. It means you want to survey a selection of the impacted employees who are going to be more representative of the general perspective and concerns that many of their peers share. Even as one is trying to get to this general perspective, it is important to avoid the iceberg concept where a single visible voice or comment represents a hidden huge mass of agreement. This is also where one may want to revisit the grassroots leaders mentioned in the previous section. However, it is important to do this in a manner that does not undermine trust others have in them. For example, it will be important to ask them what employees in general are concerned about but deliberately not attach specific names to comments. One effective way to utilize this feedback model is when one already has a sense of some of the concerns. Then you can lay these out to the grassroots leaders and let them respond with clarifications or additional details. In this model, they are validating or refuting assumptions but not actually providing extensive new information or appearing to be reporting on their peers. Then they can go back and relate the conversation in a way that others will continue to trust and confide in them.

If employees are doing well at engaging in a level of inquiry about the process of the change, then you are good to move to the next stages. However, if staff are still hung in the denial stage or clearly not convinced of the appropriateness or need for the change, then go back and assess where communications have failed and renew the active discussions described earlier in this chapter.[27] Do not be surprised if one gets feedback communicating displeasure with something that was announced a few weeks before. The manner in which an individual responds to a change will vary. Recalling the change cycle from the earlier chapter, employees may not be able to really think through a change until they have gotten past the initial denial stage. So while a manager is laying out more concrete plans and seeking input on the implementation framework, the employee is still experiencing hopeful disbelief that it will not happen. Then all of a sudden, one gets substantive valuable feedback that was needed two weeks earlier. In this scenario, it means that the leadership has moved too fast through the initial communication process and left the staff behind, contributing to disenfranchisement and a sense that one's input is not valued, thereby undermining the success of the change.

COMMUNICATING AND EMPOWERING MORE

When it comes to the last several steps of initiating the change and starting to move into the implementation process, there is a loop that one may need to go into because any change initiative is adjusted based on input. This is not to say you want people to feel pulled in every direction, but that they are apprised as the situation may be changing. Suppose you get buy-in for one part of a proposed initiative and just seem to hit a brick wall on another part of it. You go back, do an assessment, and realize that there really are problems with that part of the proposal, or the cost of pushing it through in terms of employee trust is not worth the benefit that would come from it. So as a flexible manager, you drop the piece that is problematic and go back to the drawing board with a new approach that you hope will be better and more favorably received.

At this point, it is critically important to communicate that one has modified one's plans and lay out the new direction. Otherwise, employees will still be going through the stages of change adjustment for something they do not need to consider anymore. Too much of this will lead to an emotional fatigue that emotionally wears people out. Sometimes it will require an iterative process as one is getting to a solution that meets everyone's needs and expectations. This process is one that some employees appreciate because it symbolizes that their input is appreciated and they are having an impact, which will go a long way to expanding the employees' comfort with empowerment. However, for some employees it may be too much destabilization and leave them feeling like they just stepped off of a spinning carnival ride where they cannot get their bearings. They will often communicate with phrases that reflect only wanting to know a final decision ("Just tell me what to do when it is real") or will have a strong sensitivity to perceived wasted effort ("But I just finished the analysis and now you tell me you have already decided to take a different direction"). While it is important to keep these employees informed as the details of a change initiative are evolving, they are not the ones you want to engage with heavily as grassroots leaders during this initial stage. These employees will do better within the empowerment model at a later stage of the process during the implementation and follow-up problem solving.

USING STATISTICS OR DATA WITH CARE

This was mentioned briefly earlier, but in building the premise of the need for the change, one has to use data with care. "Lies, damn lies, and statistics" is a quote that employees embrace when they feel that data has been manipulated in a way to produce the results a manager is seeking to justify a change initiative. Most people in any discipline know that statistics can be manipulated to produce the results needed.[28] If data is used heavily as the change justification, then it is critical to make it intuitive in understanding and to realize that one has to build just as strong a case for the data as one is building for the change. This is more difficult than it seems because the correlation to the research is often not clearly related to the resulting organizational change. For example, suppose social science and psychology research indicates a behavioral trend of a library population group. A leader is going to seek to develop services that support this behavior. However, the connection to the service and the desired behavior pattern may not be intuitive to library employees. Similarly, they may not see an organizational purpose to supporting the behavior. This can be particularly problematic when it pushes the institution outside of the normal service model associated with libraries. In these cases, it is important to address the philosophical disconnects early on in validating the shift. One only has to attend conference discussion forums to hear how many libraries have struggled with this in the context of social networking and mobile computing devices.

It is also important to not step in and call the data results an eye-opening revelation when staff on the front lines are sitting there saying, "Duh, if you just spent an hour at my desk you would have realized that months ago." Seeking their input based on current anecdotal perspectives can be helpful in validating the suggested change initiatives. Many times, staff and librarians on the front lines may be able to see the tree perspective but are not able to bring together the bigger pattern or picture of the forest that represents a need for change at the organizational level. Conversely, experienced managers may know less about the individual trees and more about the forest. Engaging with the staff to lead them to better understand connections between the micro and macro perspectives is an important part of building support for the change. One of the keys to applying this type of data gathering is to keep it from becoming a history-based recitation with comments like "over the last ten years . . ." or "ever since I got here 'it' was a problem." To avoid this, one needs to lead a discussion that is based on current knowledge and experiences. Similarly, it is important to keep the anecdotal comments in perspective and, in facilitating the discussions, to encourage a sense of perspective in assessing how frequently the experience occurs. To do this, one may have to challenge the staff member who includes global absolutes, such as "always," "never," "all the time," or "everyone" when describing a situation. One may also have to push for facts about something that "might" be a problem with several "if-then" circumstantial statements attached to build a realization that one is creating a worst-case scenario that will probably not happen as envisioned.

MOTIVATING ENGAGEMENT

Any modern manager knows that it is the staff who can make a significant difference to their organization when it comes to innovation, organizational change, and competitive advantage. Today managers need their employees "to be proactive and show initiative, collaborate smoothly with others, take responsibility for their own professional development, and to be committed to high quality performance standards. Thus employees are needed who feel energetic and dedicated, who are absorbed by their work. In other words, organizations need engaged workers."[29]

An engaged employee is a person who is fully involved in and enthusiastic about one's work. They are the employees who stay late in order to get something done; they go above and beyond the call of duty because they love what they are doing and care about the future of the library. However, not all employees love what they are doing and are not engaged in the organization, but rather work for the sake of a weekly paycheck. According to the semiannual Employee Engagement Index in the *Gallup Management Journal*, only 29 percent of employees are truly engaged in their position, 54 percent are not engaged, and the remaining 17 percent are actively disengaged or, more simply put, are counterproductive to what the engaged people are doing.[30] Due to this high percentage of workers who are "not engaged" in their job, leaders need to find a way to get employees to be engaged so that the organization will be able to better implement organizational change. For this reason it is believed that 29 percent of a manager's time is spent on developing motivational tactics.[31]

According to Seijts and Crim, once managers identify the current level of engagement their employees are involved at within their organizations, they must then discover motivational strategies that will help encourage their employees so that they become fully engaged in their work.[32] Discovering successful motivational strategies begins by figuring out if your employees are intrinsically or extrinsically motivated. Employees who are intrinsically motivated find their job interesting and get natural fulfillment from their job activities themselves. Employees who are extrinsically motivated, however, are not motivated by their job activity but rather by tangible rewards such as higher pay and promotion or verbal rewards which come as the consequences of completing the job.[33] However, finding ways to motivate engagement is easier said than done. It is believed that most managers do not have a precise understanding of what really motivates their employees.[34] Adding to this problem is that when employers survey their employees to see what motivates them, these surveys "generally produce results that are inconsistent with studies of actual employee behavior."[35] In looking at the importance of pay in employee motivation, there are discrepancies between what people say and what they do.[36] As a result, managers must continually search for different ways to motivate and engage so that the majority of the staff want to be a part of the change and want to give input and help move the change forward. Even if the change is so fundamentally radical that asking them to desire the change is a long shot, you want them to have some degree of trust that the change will have a positive result.

Similarly, you want to develop a culture where even if their suggestions are not applied, there is confidence that their concerns were listened to and were considered to have value and credibility. When doing this, it is important to understand where one can offer symbolic flexibility to input. If a staff sees no change between an initial model being put forward for consideration and a second stage or even a finalized one a few weeks later, there is a problem. This immediately casts doubt that the leadership is actually interested in any input. To avoid this requires the leader to set aside the grand vision idea of the completed change and be willing to make adjustments as individuals may be able to contribute. It is also important to attribute adjustments in the idea that were contributed by others to their peers. As they see input being sought and acted upon, they will be motivated to participate.

The main thing to be careful of as one is leading the initiation of a change is to avoid a negative response by trying to motivate an employee who is intrinsically motivated with extrinsically motivating strategies. At this stage of the change process, it is akin to the single freeze that can destroy an entire orchard of fruit. Unfortunately, understanding an individual's motivation and accurately triggering it can be easier said than done. Few leaders set out to de-motivate an employee, particularly when one is attempting to lead change. However, it can get frustrating and difficult to have patience while initiating change, particularly if the employees have difficulty understanding the change and are especially resistant to it for some reason. Many employees have been demoralized accidentally when the leader is overtaken by a sense of false urgency and impatience. Getting caught in this trap can lead change managers to express their frustrations in a public and personal way with comments that belittle a person's attempts at contributing. It can also lead one to gloss over suggestions on the spot, without even an appearance of consideration of the input someone might have provided. All of this will set back the ability to build buy-in to the change at this earliest stage and can undermine the success of the entire project.

KEYS TO SUCCESS

In identifying the critical issues presented in this chapter, several themes pull together in setting the stage for beginning the organizational change process. Some of these issues will be reiterated in chapter 5; however, the perspective and pitfalls will vary from a focus on talking and big-picture planning to one of details and doing.

- Avoid creating a false sense of urgency for the change that establishes a rushed timetable. Instead, allow time for the change to be understood and absorbed by individual stakeholders.
- Be willing to explain the purpose behind the change and how one got to the problem statement and proposed solution. Avoid becoming defensive as others question decisions and rationalizations in trying to reach a similar level of understanding.
- Create opportunities for active contributions and engagement to demonstrate understanding and buy-in. Avoid detailing every aspect of the grand vision at the administrative level.
- Begin building support and buy-in through grassroots allies.
- Be careful in making assumptions about what others actually understand or see as important, and avoid compartmentalizing employee responses in an absolute or superficial way.
- Take care to develop the message as customized to the individual hearing it, not how you as a manager would want or expect to hear it.

THINKING EXERCISES

1. Recall an occasion when you saw leaders introduce a change effectively to a group of stakeholders. What do you remember being most impressed by?

2. Recall an occasion when you saw leaders initiate a change poorly. Thinking of the material covered in this chapter, what did they do wrong?

3. If you were to implement a change in your department, who would you identify as your grassroots change leaders and why?

4. Think of a change you would like to make in your department. What different methods and approaches would you use to introduce the change to the employees? How long do you think it would take to build a majority buy-in for the change?

NOTES

1. Larry R. Smeltzer, "An Analysis of Strategies for Announcing Organizational-Wide Change," *Group and Organizational Studies* 16, no. 1 (1991): 5–24.
2. Mike Green, *Change Management Masterclass: A Step by Step Guide to Successful Change* (Philadelphia: Kogan Page, 2007).
3. Ibid.
4. Philip J. Kitchen and Finbarr Daly, "Internal Communication during Change Management," *Corporate Communications* 7, no. 1 (2002): 46–53.
5. Paul Strebel, "Why Do Employees Resist Change?" *Harvard Business Review* 74 (May–June 1996): 86–92.
6. Ibid.
7. Alper Erturk, "A Trust-Based Approach to Promote Employees' Openness to Organizational Change in Turkey," *International Journal of Manpower* 29, no. 5 (2008): 462–83.
8. Kitchen and Daly, "Internal Communication during Change Management."
9. John P. Kotter, "Leading Change: Why Transformation Efforts Fail," *Harvard Business Review* 73, no. 2 (1995): 59–67.
10. Laurie K. Lewis and others, "Advice on Communicating during Organizational Change," *Journal of Business Communication* 43, no. 2 (2006): 113–37.
11. V. Nilakant and S. Ramnarayan, *Change Management: Altering Mindset in a Global Context* (California: Sage, 2006), 168.
12. Ming-Chu Yu, "Employees' Perception of Organizational Change: The Mediating Effects of Stress Management Strategies," *Public Personnel Management* 38, no. 1 (2009): 17–32.
13. Shel Holtz, *Corporate Conversations: A Guide to Crafting Effective and Appropriate Internal Communications* (New York: Amacom, 2004).
14. Elizabeth Wolfe Morrison and Frances J. Milliken, "Organizational Silence: A Barrier to Change and Development in a Pluralistic World," *Academy of Management Review* 25, no. 4 (October 2000): 706–25.
15. C. J. Nemeth, "Managing Innovation: When Less Is More," *California Management Review* 40, no. 1 (1997): 59–74; Kathleen D. Ryan and Daniel K. Oestreich, *Driving*

Fear Out of the Workplace: How to Overcome the Invisible Barriers to Quality, Productivity and Innovation (San Francisco: Jossey-Bass, 1991).

16. Morrison and Milliken, "Organizational Silence."
17. Nilakant and Ramnarayan, *Change Management,* 162.
18. Lewis and others, "Advice on Communicating during Organizational Change."
19. Sergio Fernandez and Hal G. Rainey, "Managing Successful Organizational Change in the Public Sector," *Public Administration Review* (March/April 2006): 168–76.
20. Ibid.
21. Nilakant and Ramnarayan, *Change Management,* 166.
22. Kotter, "Leading Change."
23. Manuela Pardo del Val and Clara Martinez Fuentes, "Resistance to Change: A Literature Review and Empirical Study," *Journal of Management Decision* 41, no. 2 (2003): 148–55; Sandy Kristin Piderit, "Rethinking Resistance and Recognizing Ambivalence: A Multidimensional View of Attitudes Toward an Organizational Change," *Academy of Management* 25, no. 4 (2000): 783–94.
24. Kotter, "Leading Change."
25. Nilakant and Ramnarayan, *Change Management,* 158.
26. Kotter, "Leading Change."
27. Vivien Swanson and Kevin Power, "Employees' Perceptions of Organizational Restructuring: The Role of Social Support," *Work & Stress* 15, no. 2 (2001): 161–78.
28. Lisa C. Heinz, "White Lies, Damned Lies and Statistics," *Engineering and Science* (Fall 1989): 19–23; Christine M. Anderson-Cook, "More Damned Lies and Statistics: How Numbers Confuse Public Issues/Change: A Guide to Gambling, Love, the Stock Market, & Just About Everything Else," *American Statistician* 59, no. 3 (2005): 274–75: Derek Roger, "Psychometrics: Lies, Damn Lies, and Statistics?" *Human Resources Magazine* 14, no. 2 (2009): 16–17.
29. Arnold Bakker and Wilmar Schaufeli, "Positive Organizational Behavior: Engaged Employees in Flourishing Organizitions," *Journal of Organizational Behavior* 29, no. 2 (2008): 147–54.
30. Beverly Little and Philip Little, "Employee Engagement: Conceptual Issues," *Journal of Organizational Culture, Communications and Conflict* 10, no. 1 (2006): 111–20.
31. P. Hise, "Chart Showing Amounts of Time CEOs Spend on Various Human-Resources Issues," *Motivation Inclination Inc.* 15, no. 8 (1993): 28.
32. Gerard H. Seijts and Dan Crim, "What Engages Employees the Most, or, The Ten C's of Employee Engagement," *Ivery Business Journal* (March/April 2006): 1–5.
33. Marylène Gagné and Edward L. Deci, "Self-Determination Theory and Work Motivation," *Journal of Organizational Behavior* 26 (2005): 331–62.
34. Carole L. Jurkiewicz, Tom K. Massey, and Roger G. Brown, "Motivation in Public and Private Organizations: A Comparative Study," *Public Productivity and Management Review* 21, no. 3 (1998): 230–50.
35. Sara L. Rynes, Barry Gerhart, and Kathleen A. Minette, "The Importance of Pay in Employee Motivation: Discrepancies Between What People Say and What They Do," *Human Resource Management* 43, no. 4 (2004): 381.
36. Ibid., 381–94.

CHAPTER 5 ————————————————————————————

IMPLEMENTING CHANGE EFFECTIVELY

To effectively communicate, we must realize that we are all different in the way we perceive the world and use this understanding as a guide to our communication with others.

—Anthony Robbins

NOW THAT YOU have done the critical preliminary work to understand resistance, build acceptance, and create buy-in to the idea of the change, it is finally time to actually carry out the change implementation process. Many changes have failed because managers and administrators have jumped immediately from a basic announcement of the change to this stage. The primary reason for this failure is because some change managers do not sufficiently consider their organizational environment, which causes them to neglect key variables of the fundamental structure of their organization. Not only must the change leader understand why the organization needs to change but how the change will affect the organization itself. Understanding how the organization will be affected by the change can be achieved only by analyzing department interactions to identify areas of interdependence and resistance within the organization. This will give the manager knowledge of who will be affected by the change and how they will be affected.[1] Having this prior knowledge before implementation will give the change leader the ability to forecast and deal with potential difficulties earlier in the change process and remove potential difficulties before implementation begins.[2] In truth, implementation should almost be the anticlimactic part of the process as individuals are immersed in the details of making the change happen. That is not to say it is without drama. There will always be the incident where someone speaks up in a meeting and says with bewilderment, "This wasn't what I intended when I supported the idea," despite one's best efforts to communicate the intention of the change. This is because as much as one has laid out a vision of the change, that vision is interpreted through filters, and it is only as the change is implemented that the vision becomes reality. As the cliché goes, the devil is in the details. However, if one has laid the groundwork appropriately, the confused or surprised employee will be the exception rather than the norm.

Similarly, as much as one tries to anticipate and plan for things, foresight is never as clear as hindsight and there will always be something that comes up to disrupt plans. The W. W. Hagerty Library of Drexel University, for example, faced unexpected disruptions to its plan to migrate from a print journal collection to an electronic journal collection. The change leaders at the Hagerty Library knew that the move toward an electronic journal collection would change the skills needed in the serials acquisitions unit, but the library did not expect nor were they prepared for an increased need for skilled professional staff to manage the new electronic serials collection. In addition, the library was unexpectedly forced to change the fundamental way its public service areas operated because of the format change.[3] Some disruptions will be minimal and within one's control for crisis management, while others may rock the entire project and require one to step back to the initiation stage and revisit alternatives. Although stepping back and revisiting alternatives is a must for change leaders, the perceived instability can cause additional anxiety for those staff members who dislike change. Addressing the unexpected disruption is discussed more in chapter 6.

During the implementation stage it is important to provide training and coaching in order to facilitate positive results. Training your staff is necessary if they are required to perform new job duties that demand a more complex set of skills. Training will also reduce employees' change-resistant attitudes, since the change becomes more familiar. In addition to training, coaching is also an important factor during the implementation process. Effective coaching increases staff members' motivation favorably toward change and helps get them to align with the needs of the organization. It is during the implementation phase that real-time feedback can be gained from employees, since the change is no longer "theory-based" but now is actually happening. Staff will no longer be sitting on the sidelines attempting to visualize the described change but are now active members of the change team. One important point to remember about training is that not all people learn at the same pace in the same way. That is why it is important to allow people to learn at their own pace and provide them opportunities for guided, hands-on, experiential training in addition to lectures or help guides. Flexible timing can also be important for training. Some staff members are comfortable with last-minute training right before a process change is implemented. Others need training ahead of time and the opportunity to do practice exercises as part of the preparation. One key aspect is to construct the training in a way that it is relevant to the individual's job.[4] These are all part of the primary responsibility of the change leader: keeping the project pointed toward the destination and maintaining positive engagement on the part of the employees impacted by the change.

GUIDING WITHOUT DRIVING

According to Harrison and Pratt, implementing a full-scale change within an organization requires the organization to assign change accountabilities to front-line managers and set targets and timetables for actions and improvements.[5] Within most organizations there are three specific layers of management thinking, though a specific organization may have more than one reporting line within a specific layer. The top managers develop the organization's vision, mission, and strategic long-term plans and incorporate broad change initiatives. Within academic libraries, top managers often correspond to deans and associate deans or directors. The middle managers are those who give life to the top managers' strategies and directives by developing operational plans. They are most frequently identified as the "change leaders." Within many libraries, middle managers would correspond to individual department heads or large team leaders. The front-line managers are those managers who actually implement operational plans and engage in the daily work, processes, and changes required to satisfy middle- and upper-management proposals.[6] Within libraries, these will often be assistant department heads or senior supervisors within the unit. However, depending on the size and organizational structure of a specific library, its managerial leadership style and operational staffing roles can blur between the levels. This blurring can occur if there is a need to "translate" the vision from the manager to the employee, and it can also occur during the planning and implementing stages. The key is to remember that the manager's role is to effectively manage and implement the change process, not to define or control every aspect of it.[7]

However, even as the various management levels are responsible for planning and implementing the change, it is important that middle managers keep their instincts to take control in check as the implementation process begins. Even as one may have a clear vision of the perfect way the plan should be implemented and be impatient to reach the end results, the path is not immediately intuitive to everyone impacted by the change, including the front-line manager. As an analogy, compare the actions of a guide who is leading a group on a hiking adventure with a rancher trying to move a herd to a different pasture with better grass. In both cases, the guide or rancher has to set a reasonable pace that the group as a whole can keep, but he must also keep the group intact and not lose group members. The group, be it hikers or members of a herd, may find it hard work in going from one place to another, and sometimes it is even a nervous experience as one is taken out of one's comfort zone. The key difference in these two examples is the impact of the experience on the subject and what the motivation is for moving. In the case of the hiking adventure, there is opportunity for it to be a learning experience for the participants. For the rancher, the herd may be happy once they start eating the greener grass, but the experience of getting there offers little actual growth. Similarly, guides will sometimes say that they are revitalized by the discovery process of seeing the sights through someone else's eyes for the first time and learn something new from every group they lead. This generally is not the case for the relationship between the cowboy and the herd.

These analogies may be a bit exaggerated, but serve to make the point that the implementation needs to continue to be an area where the change manager is engaging with the employees in a way that is a mutually rewarding experience with opportunities for learning. Bartunek and others describe how an organization discovered that the changes they needed to implement in order to stay competitive in today's market were going to change the fundamental way the company did its day-to-day business.[8] As a result, during the implementation process, the company's employees were encouraged by the administration to learn about the change, and to do this they needed to become involved in the implementation process. Everyone from the materials personnel, assemblers, and testers to supervisors learned about the change by participating in the diagnosis, analysis, and feedback that resulted in the implementation of the change. This allowed employees to translate the organizational goals into their own vernacular and own them during the implementation process. In order to accomplish a change in this manner, the effective change manager has to focus on guiding employees, with the path taken being seen of equal importance to the end result achieved. This requires one to offer options and be willing to change plans in response to legitimate interest and engagement. To return to our previous analogy, suppose the guide learns that several members of the group are avid bird watchers but are not too interested in watching mammals. This might mean that instead of setting up camp near a pasture on a moose trail, it would be better to camp among the trees where there are a wide variety of bird species. Change leaders also need to adjust the pace and path being set to accomplish a particular change. Suppose that one is leading a unit reorganization. One may find that the staff members would rather spend more time discussing what their position responsibilities will be in the new structure rather than which supervisor they report to on the organizational chart, or vice versa. Though both may be important, one may be where the impacted employees want to linger and have more thoughtful and engaged dialogue about the final outcome, or need more time to adjust to it. It is important to remember that although organizational change is rewarding to some, it will not be for all. The reason for this is because organizational change runs contrary to the human need for consistency and stability. As a result, the change agent must walk a fine line between stability and change.[9]

If a change manager tends to employ a driver approach, it is very easy to get caught up with a sense of false urgency or a need to control the situation once the implementation begins. This can lead a change manager to force implementation decisions and actions to an artificial timeline that does not allow for opportunities to effectively engage with employees for optimal shared problem solving and effective decision making. This is not to say that a guide does not also have a target deadline, but that deadline is in part set by the individuals taking part in the hike. They have determined in the initial discussions and negotiations whether this is a day hike or a two-week adventure and have come to agreement with the guide on the goals expected of the hike. This same process should be part of the implementation process, with impacted staff members being a part of the discussion on the implementation's timing and pace. The purpose of the manager is to ensure that forward progress is made but not to establish all the parameters in a vacuum. It is important to remember that no one individual can create a successful change process. Implementing successful change can occur only when a group of employees bring together their collective organizational knowledge to create the change.[10]

TWO-WAY COMMUNICATION

According to Stober, despite a change manager's best efforts an employee may relapse, in which case the individual falls back into old behavior patterns of resisting change.[11] This is why it is important that leaders continue to promote two-way communications with their staff members and have a comprehensive strategic communication plan as part of the ongoing implementation, in order to provide them with the data they need to support their internal struggle to create change.[12] Although the change manager has been communicating the change throughout the process, it does not stop during the implementation process. According to Lippitt and others, "From the moment someone senses a need for change until long after the final crossing of the last 'T' in a summary report of accomplishment—by far the most important element contributing to success is the art and act of communicating."[13]

Even as the change manager makes efforts to engage with impacted employees and make them part of the implementation process, employees need to be encouraged and held accountable to be active and effective participants. As employees speak up, several patterns will emerge. It is natural for managers to enjoy and appreciate employees who have enthusiastically bought in to the change and are ready to implement it immediately as the manager has laid it out. However, often this will be only a small subset of the employees involved in the change. A larger number of employees will react in a more guarded, perceptually unconvinced or even negative manner, which can actually be more valuable to the manager. One key factor to successfully implementing change is dealing constructively with employees who hold different views. It is important for change leaders to recognize and distinguish between the hostile employee who is using the guise of empowerment to undermine or hold back progress on a change, the engaged employee who is struggling with understanding the breadth or depth of a change, and the supportive employee who has identified problems with the implementation that could derail the change. While the first group cannot be ignored, most of one's efforts as a change leader should go to engagement with the latter groups. According to Hedge and Pulakos, when any type of change implementation occurs it is likely to clash with individual organizational interests and internal organizational alliances.[14] This is why it is important to make sure to sustain two-way communication: it is a key to recognizing the difference between active change sabotage and natural change resistance. It can also help one realize when an idea is challenged whether the individual employee is hostile to the change or just uses a "problem solver" approach that tends to need to pick apart an idea before finding the best implementation path. The latter is often mislabeled as a problem, change-resistant employee when the problem is actually a disconnect in communication and implementation styles. According to Gallagher and others, it is important for the change manager to "consider resistance as a force protecting something of value in the organization. Engage the resistance and access whether the specific component that is being valued is an element that needs to be incorporated into the change implementation plans."[15]

Because they are the most visible, one may wonder how a change leader should address the actively hostile employees in a way that does not consume one's time and energies. There are a couple of different approaches depending on one's personal communication style and comfort in managing conflict; the key is not to dismiss these employees, but rather to value those who are showing signs of resistance to change. To do this one can try to work directly with individuals or work through supervisors to understand and address their concerns. Do they think the decision will undermine the library's primary role in meeting a user's information needs? If so, why? By getting to the last question, one can look for middle ground that will move the employee away from the hostile posture. Suppose in a discussion with a hostile employee about changing the responsibilities for processing microforms, the employee raises concerns that services will suffer because the new people will not know enough. At this point, one can acknowledge the validity of the concern and respond by empowering the individual to play an active part in the solution, such as having the person take responsibility in developing a training program and guides that teach the new employee what they need to know. One can also ask employees to suspend their skepticism or resistance for a time to give you the opportunity to prove or disprove the concept.

At some point, one may have to take a harder approach and be more directive by establishing what are the true non-negotiables in the changing situation. This may mean setting a deadline to get an employee moving or making decisions that will clearly establish accountability on the part of the employee to begin engaging. Even when doing this, it is important to keep a door open to be willing to meet employees part way as they begin to struggle toward accepting the change and engaging with it. In the worst cases, one may have to simply move forward and marginalize the hostile employee and simply ignore the negativity and heckling. One may want to address the inability to move forward in an evaluation only if the resistance has had an actual impact on the employee's performance. Attempting to put someone into a disciplinary process or deny a raise based on employee attitude is a slippery legal slope, particularly if one is at a larger institution with prescribed evaluation standards. The last thing a leader wants to do is set up a situation where others feel sorry for the employee, or provide an opportunity for the employee to stall the change with grievance or lawsuit processes.

These harder approaches will work so long as one follows the first guideline of putting the majority of one's energies in bringing along those that are more open to the change but struggling with the details or personal implications of the change. This is where empowerment will have the greatest impact. If one has invested energies in bringing everyone else on board to the change, the hostile employee will end up losing their support and respect and will be viewed with scorn or pity for maintaining such an intractable position.

BUY-IN THROUGH EMPOWERMENT

As stated in previous chapters, empowering employees to help lead change is vital to the success of the change process. Many employees will be less likely to resist change and more engaged in moving a change forward if they have the opportunity to give real input and take an active part in the process in order to have a visible impact on how the change is carried forward.[16] Empowerment is the key to unlocking employees' potential vigor, knowledge, and abilities. Managers can foster this by creating an infrastructure that gives the employees an opportunity to make meaningful suggestions. However, in addition to making sure there is opportunity to give input and creating a culture where employees feel they can speak up, managers have to be willing to check their own preconceived ideas at the door. This means that the manager or change leader cannot plan out every detail beforehand and must acknowledge that there may be equally valid paths of getting to the end result that an employee can contribute. One must deliberately leave some aspects of the implementation plan in an amorphous or undecided state and then hand off the undecided aspects to the employees to add the details on. By engaging employees in active participation in the implementation process, the change manager is also continually building the employees' commitment not only to the implementation process but also to the company's values, goals, purpose, and principles.[17] This often takes managers out of their comfort zones because it is offering up control to someone else, and employees may come up with something totally different than what the manager was expecting to be the successful model.[18] A good technique to cope with this balance between manager and empowered employees is to have both work together to come up with a set of expectations and establish a "boundary of power." As they build trust in each other over time, this boundary can be expanded.[19] In addition, as problems that a change-leading manager did not anticipate are identified, the change leader must avoid undermining the empowerment. This is done by demonstrating flexibility to ideas and listening to the employees' concerns without responding defensively or feeling that one's efforts to move the project along are not being appreciated. Empowerment will often increase the implementation time, but ultimately saves time later in revising the plan to accommodate issues of concern identified by the impacted employees during implementation. This will be easier to do if one has already worked to establish a culture that allows for adjustments as a project moves along rather than expecting perfection from the start. The culture also needs to allow for a bad idea to be abandoned or adjusted away from the original vision, something leaders who have already emotionally invested in an idea's success can struggle with accepting. Empowering does not mean that the change manager gives up all control of the initiative or ceases monitoring the progress of the change taking place. As Haevey states, nothing works on automatic pilot for long, and as a result, without the change manager monitoring the process and nurturing the plans along, the change initiative will falter.[20] The key is to know when it is necessary to step out in front and pull the employee up the mountain, when to walk alongside the employee as you both take part in the adventure, and when to let the employee lead while you follow close behind.

According to Leban and Stone, there are nine key motivators of employees that can be used in an empowered environment:[21]

1. Material rewards—seeking possessions, wealth, and a high standard of living

2. Power/influence—seeking to be in control of people and resources

3. Search for meaning—seeking to do things that are believed valuable for their own sake

4. Expertise—seeking a high level of accomplishment in a specialized field

5. Creativity—seeking to innovate and be identified with original output

6. Affiliation—seeking nourishing relationships with others

7. Autonomy—seeking to be independent and able to make decisions for oneself

8. Security—seeking a solid and predictable future

9. Status—seeking to be recognized, admired, and respected by the community at large

However, the key to using these motivators is that their results must support the overall goals of the organization, and when used together Leban and Stone believe they will help create a network of support for implementing change within the organization.

While many managers probably feel they already empower employees during the change implementation process, their employees may feel differently. One should look closely at one's empowerment strategies to make sure they are effective. In some cases, managers have chosen areas of empowerment that have such little actual impact that the employees feel they are being assigned busywork that is pointless. For an empowered environment to exist, an employee's position or role must have two key components: core expectations of the basic job description that an employee must accomplish; and job flexibility so that employees can use their competence and interest to move change forward. According to Leban and Stone, this does not mean individuals cannot work together to accomplish something.[22] "Job overlap, rather than being avoided, becomes an opportunity for sharing information and innovation."[23] Another empowerment pitfall will occur when managers have a mental image that they are already planning to impose if the employee's suggested plan does not match it. This situation becomes a guessing game as employees search to find the "right" answer that gets them a "happy face" from the boss rather than a frown. Employees in these situations will quickly give up on trying to contribute to the implementation process because they do not feel it will have any impact on the final plan or it is simply too frustrating to try and intuit what the change leader has already decided is the best path to follow.

So what does real empowerment look like? It gives employees the freedom to actually make decisions or see the impact of their comments through changes in the implementation process. One key in using empowerment is to avoid letting one vocal employee usurp the empowerment of others, either unintentionally through natural assertiveness or deliberately in having a personal agenda. To avoid this, change leaders need to run suggestions past others for endorsement or denial. One may not be able to achieve a consensus agreement, but having pushed the conversations and letting individuals see there was or was not support for their suggestion still serves as a positive example of empowerment. In truth, some employees struggle with the concept of empowerment because it requires them to share in the accountability of the success of the project. Some may feel uncomfortable in publicly engaging in conflict with a peer that they have to continue to work with over the long term. This is particularly an issue in a multicultural workforce where individuals may have a cultural filter that inhibits their comfort in speaking up because of gender, age, or rank/status issues. In these situations, a change leader will need to engage with individuals on a one-on-one basis in a "safe" environment. This means that small teams may need to be put together in the context of interpersonal skills and leadership strengths or weaknesses. It may also be important to conduct some training in listening and facilitation. Finally, there may need to be points during the implementation process where a change leader has to carve out the time to literally meet with each employee primarily impacted by the change and assess their progress toward buy-in and address unvoiced concerns. After holding these meetings, one can stand up in front of the group and announce support or disagreement with some issues that were raised previously. A desired outcome of these meetings is that the employee is encouraged to move beyond a lack of understanding of the theoretical change to being interested in the change and even wanting the change to occur. If the change manager is lucky, employees will feel more comfortable with their empowerment roles to finally want to take action in implementing the change.[24]

In order to achieve the desired outcome, it is important when holding these one-on-one meetings to have a consistent starting structure for each one. A preference is for the meeting to take place in some location other than the manager's office, but if that is the only place to hold the meetings, the manager should work to make the interaction a comfortable one for the employee that minimizes the authority structure of the relationship. This reduces the perceptual "meeting with the boss" effect on an employee and sends a message of equity and fairness. The structure needs to clearly open dialogue in a nonthreatening way that gives an employee some icebreaker time. One way to accomplish this is to start the discussion with a preset group of questions that each employee can think about beforehand and prepare for. Questions should be open-ended in a way that encourages dialogue and can range from straightforward to sophisticated. One thing to avoid in these meetings is to ask for someone's opinion or observation about another employee. Unless handled very carefully, this can undermine trust and can lead managers astray in their understanding of a situation. Some examples of effective starter questions might include:

What do you think is going right in the way we are implementing the [name] project?

What do you think is a problem in the way we are implementing the [name] project?

What concerns or issues do you have about the [name] project? (Note: It is better to ask what concerns the employee has rather than asking what questions the employee has because a person might not have any questions, but when in a change situation, employees *always* have some type of concern.)

What do you think about the progress we are making?

What do you think will be the biggest challenge or barrier to the [name] project's success?

Why do you think the initiative will or will not work?

How do you feel about the suggestion/recommendation that we should be doing [x]? (Note: This question will get at the vocal minority concern mentioned earlier.)

By using questions that provide the content for further discussion, the change leader can elicit a customized conversation that captures valuable information for further enhancing buy-in and understanding employee needs during the implementation process.

BALANCING NEEDS

Even as change leaders work to understand the employees' needs during the implementation of a major organizational change, it is also part of their role to recognize the
institution's needs and balance between the two. For many employees, their individual
needs may simply be incompatible with the big picture. It can be a challenge to keep
employees engaged when they perceive their individual needs being overwhelmed
by the organization's needs. As an example, suppose a work team does not want to
get split up or combined with another group of staff because of fear of overwork or
past conflict. However, the resource needs of the organization indicate that combining the staff will result in significant cost-saving measures. In this case, one can put
extra energies into rebuilding a respectful relationship between the employees in
the two groups, promising to monitor the situation so that potential problems are
addressed in a timely manner while still minor. Generally, one cannot let a personal
reluctance to engage or take on different responsibilities hold back a change that will
have an institution-wide benefit. The exception to this is where the culture issues are
so deeply embedded and problematic that the cost-saving measure will be negated
by the managerial resources cost of constantly mediating conflict. In this situation,
it may be better to look for a middle ground, a lengthier staged implementation, or a
compromise alternative.

In addition, managers must keep an eye on the implementation groups to make sure
they are not feeling lost because they have forgotten what their purpose is. Curzon
believes that "loss of purpose is one of the most common reasons for change disintegration."[25] This happens when a group gets lost in the process of implementation
and the overall purpose of the implementation process begins to falter. This generally
happens when the change implementation process is too large for the group to do in
the short deadline given to implement it. The implementation team is faced with too
much data, and the complexity of the project becomes overwhelming. The team will
become tired and frustrated with the implementation process and can in time become
a hindrance to the process. It is important for the administration to remember that
in order to achieve an optimal change implementation, changes must occur one at a
time. Too much change all at once, especially if the changes are interdependent or
actually contradict each other, will cause confusion, frustration, and failure. With each
additional overlaid change initiative, the likelihood of implementing the changes successfully goes down. Later chapters discuss staging complex, multiple, or overlapping
changes in a way that is less overwhelming for the stakeholders, but ultimately it may
be important to realize that one is dealing with individuals who have emotional and
physical limits and can be burned out if pushed too hard.

Lost implementation teams are a situation where change managers truly refine their leadership skills in addressing concerns while still moving the project forward. This may require a broad tool set of interpersonal and conflict management skills, from the direct, matter-of-fact approach to a sympathetic but firm negotiation style. It may even be necessary to adopt different styles when dealing with the same employee but on different issues of concern. This is part of the reason why change leadership is the ultimate challenge in situational leadership. For someone who has been reading this chapter, this is where you may be saying, "Wait a minute, earlier the emphasis was on flexibility and empowering the individual and letting them set the pace . . ." This is why this section's heading focuses on *balance*. Often a change manager must work through competing priorities and agendas at the individual and the organizational levels when implementing a major organizational change. The real trick is to do so in a way that lets neither perspective become the dominating one. Like two children on a seesaw, you do not want to leave either the individual or the organization hanging in the air. Instead, one wants to recognize where one or the other has flexibility in adopting various aspects or stages of the change.

PAYING ATTENTION TO THE SMALL STUFF

With apologies to Richard Carlson, author of *Don't Sweat the Small Stuff,* when leading a change in the implementation stages, the small stuff can make or break the timely success of the initiative. Most employees will not set out to deliberately undermine or abandon a project. However, because they are expending a lot of emotional energy in just adapting to the idea of a change initiative, they are easily disillusioned or sidetracked when running into barriers or challenges on small or large issues, which is discussed more in chapter 6. Employees who would normally be great troubleshooters may be distracted enough in adapting to the change that they become easily frustrated. Earlier sections mentioned engaging with front-line employees and listening to their concerns. Because they are immersed in the day-to-day activities, they are the ones who have the best sense of the small details and can identify the negative impacts of change. Those employees who work "where the rubber meets the road" have the best vantage point to see how the changed goals will affect the library. They need to be able to communicate their concerns, no matter how small, to upper management, and these concerns need to be considered and responded to during the implementation process in order for the library to reach their desired results. As Spector points out, "Employees possess 'local knowledge' about customers, competitors, and how the products and services of the organization meet the shifting needs of the marketplace that need to be communicated upward in the organization."[26] Change leaders focused on motivating employees can find it tedious when every conversation opens with something identified as a barrier to change at the minutia level. However, brushing past the minutia undermines employee buy-in and quickly leads to important details getting overlooked that can imperil the later success of the project. There is nothing worse than to have planned an office layout redesign and then discover that no one talked to tech support about activating new Internet ports or relocating the computers while the furniture is being deconstructed. Similarly, a basic ADA-compatible aisle may look great on paper until one realizes it will need to accommodate a steady traffic of loaded book trucks and provides inadequate bending and reaching space in front of the on-hold bookshelf.

So who is responsible for the small stuff? This is where having established an empowerment model for employee engagement will pay the greatest rewards. An excellent example of this is when the CEO of the United Services Automobile Association, Robert McDermott, pushed decision-making authority down to lower-level employees relating to customer service.[27] With the majority of the workforce positively engaged on the change and bringing the small stuff to the forefront so it would not be overlooked, the change manager can subsequently delegate back to the employees follow-up responsibilities so the small stuff is addressed. This can include putting in help desk requests for IT support or talking to the facilities manager about using a wider aisle standard. Because the employee brought up the concern, he will be less likely to let it slip through the cracks as the change leader might because the change leader is mimicking the role of a juggler who is keeping many balls in the air. Often when an employee will bring up what seems like a minute element of the overall plan, the employee has some idea of the appropriate action "someone" should be taking but just needs reassurance that he is the appropriate "someone."

Even as one is delegating the minutia, it is the responsibility of the change manager to keep the overall plan in sight and not get sidetracked into taking ownership of too many of the small details or letting the need to resolve small details prevent overall success. While knowledge and awareness of the details are valuable, the leader's role is to not let the project get derailed while everyone else tries to anticipate every possible scenario or possibility that might need to be addressed. For example, suppose a library is changing a fine model or adding graphic novels to the collection. Employees can throw up a tremendous number of "what if" statements. For some of the statements, there may be clear answers. For others, the "answer" should be one where the leader encourages having a plan in the event the "what if" comes true, but not let the fear of what might happen derail the project. Having helped develop a culture of risk taking and then responding effectively to unexpected events will help establish a mindset where "what if" is asked in a contemplative, problem-solving mode rather than a fearful mode that seeks an answer from someone else. One can also respond to the fearful "what if" in a matter-of-fact tone that says, "We will deal with that if it happens but there is no guarantee that it will come true." In doing this, it is important to choose one's words carefully so that employees know they were listened to and that they are not being marginalized, but that their concern has an equal chance of not happening as it does of happening. In this case, the unit will have gone through the mental exercise in how to address the situation and can move on.

STAYING FLEXIBLE

If readers are feeling that implementing change is a balancing act or tug-of-war between details and the big picture, they are not far off. There is no magic formula that defines when a change leader has to get involved with details and when they can be successfully delegated. However, as stated above, monitoring the implementation process is the key. In complex change, such as a large space reorganization, it is inevitable that at some point the change manager will delegate something that falls through a crack or goes awry, making one wish one had stayed on top of the details. Also, one may think everything is under control and the change is moving forward when leaving the office on a Friday and walk in to a Monday morning conversation that indicates everyone left a meeting with a totally different perspective of what is going to happen when and to whom. For this reason, the most important tool in the change manager's toolkit is the ability to stay flexible and adjust as needed by responding in a situational leadership model that can quickly assess a situation and take the best action to address the problem. Like Colin Powell stated: "There are no secrets to success. It is the result of preparation, hard work, and learning from failure."[28] When working in this model, the last thing change leaders should waste their energies on is assigning fault or blame or ranting against fate or misfortune. Instead managers need to make a conscious decision on what to do when their expectations for change implementation have not been met.

Implementation problems, particularly environmental factors, can come from a variety of sources and will be discussed in more detail in chapter 6. Sometimes the change manager's need for flexibility to respond effectively will be called up by something that was not anticipated, such as removing flooring or paint and discovering asbestos or lead contaminants. On other occasions, it will come from having simply misjudged a response to a problem. Suppose an academic library decides to change how study rooms are checked out to patrons, thinking it will solve a known problem with late key returns and shift accountability to the students. However, the change leaders and staff misjudge the students' response to the change. Subsequently, the comment box overflows with complaints on how the students find the new system to be even worse and unacceptable in meeting their needs. In this case, one has to be willing to accept that the change did not work and go back to the drawing board in the hope of finding a better compromise solution that addresses both the original problem and the newly introduced problem.[29] In other cases, the disruption to the change initiative will come from events that were totally beyond one's control. Suppose one is engaged in doing an academic library renovation project. Everything is on schedule, but then the sprinkler system malfunctions in a large classroom building, flooding it. At this point all campus facility support resources, staff, and materials are going to get reprioritized to deal with the sprinkler disaster, and one may not even know the impact on the schedule of the in-progress library renovation project for several weeks. Finally, though crises such as the ones previously described can occur, many implementation breakdowns revolve around a communication failure.

When dealing with a communication failure, trying to assign responsibility is a futile effort that can only undermine employee engagement and empowerment. Instead accept that something is broken and take action to move it forward. One can analyze the "why" of the communication breakdown at a later time. One example of a common communication failure comes in what can be called "flipping the switch." Suppose a process is being changed. Everyone has bought into the change occurring, and the manager closes the last planning meeting with a comment about being good to go with the new process and mentally moves on to the next initiative. In the manager's mind, having been immersed in the project, this phrasing means to make the change now. However, employees are often waiting for a definitive statement such as "Make the change effective 8 a.m. Monday." Without bringing closure to the implementation process, the manager is destined to walk in a few weeks later and discover the employees are still using the old process and waiting for official word on when to change to the new process. At this point it does no one any good to get mad, though a little exasperation would not be untoward. The key thing is to verify that everyone is ready to go and send out an e-mail saying one has discovered there was some confusion and tomorrow at 8 a.m. staff will implement the operational changes.

KEEP COMMUNICATING

In staying flexible to respond to communication breakdowns during the implementation, it is important to keep communicating with all the stakeholders about the progress of the change. Managers must remember that even during the implementation process when events seem transparent, communications such as status reports on progress and accomplishments can still be distorted by the sender or receiver of the message. One example of this is when people omit information from a message because they believe the information's audience should already know that information, and as a result they do not send the needed data to support a decision. In addition, managers must remember that the message's language itself is very important. Nelson states that "because most words have several meanings, some people will interpret a message one way and some another."[30] As a result, when sending out communications, it is important to provide information about any developing initiatives related to the change, updates on some minute-level changes to the original plan, and reminders of things to be aware of. In order to avoid misinterpretation of the message's language, the person sending the message must keep it professional, clear, complete, and concise. Nelson suggests that one "use short words and short sentences. Ask several people to review important messages before they are transmitted to the receivers to be sure that the main points are unambiguous."[31] Additionally, using just one medium for communication—weekly/monthly unit meetings, e-mail, one-on-one, and so on—is inadequate because information unfolds on its own timetable and is absorbed and processed by different people in different ways. While the one-on-one method is probably the most effective, few change leaders have the time to meet frequently with each employee. Sometimes it may be necessary to work through supervisors, which always introduces the potential of inaccuracies through additional information filters. One also needs to customize communication to the audience. An administrator probably will not want all of the minute details that front-line staff need. In fact, if one is engaging with an administrator on the details, one should not be surprised to be met with confusion and a request to explain why something is "important." By contrast, many front-line employees want to immerse themselves in the details, and trying to provide a broad overview will result in a deluge of "Why?" and "But wait, did you consider . . . ?" questions. The one thing to remember is that few change leaders are criticized for overcommunicating to all audiences. One may want to acknowledge in opening remarks that some have already heard the information and be tolerant as they may be less attentive, possibly multitasking with a mobile computing device. One caution is to stay consistent as you communicate to different groups and allow individuals that hear the information in one forum to opt out of hearing it again in another meeting.

Referring back to the previous flooded classroom example, one might wonder how much detail about the situation needs to be shared with the front-line staff engaged in the project. The answer is that more detail is always better so long as one remembers that employees are individuals with different personal needs for information receipt and filtering. For every employee who wants to hear why there is going to be a two-week delay in the completion of the ductwork, there may be another who has gotten what he needs to hear in your opening statement, that there will be a two-week delay. The thing to remember is that if you do not provide the details for those who wonder "why," they will speculate and imagine scenarios that sidetrack the energies of others. This will have a subsequent impact on their ability to focus on the other aspects of implementing the change. By anticipating the speculation and providing an official "report," even if the report is that "we don't have an answer yet," employees engaged in change will stay more engaged in the implementation process and immersed in the details of continuing to move the change along.

EVALUATING PROGRESS AND SUCCESS

From the previous sections on flexibility and balance a change leader may be wondering how any progress gets made for a change to be successful. In truth, many carefully planned changes are successful with only a few disruptions to the schedule, which can be dealt with in a straightforward manner. The key is to continue to make progress even when one is faced with the particularly difficult change initiative that seems to meet challenges every day with a wide range of staff members. Some changes will be very popular and most of the employees will be enthusiastic about the change. Others are less popular, and asking for a positive, enthusiastic response may just not be realistic. In this case, one may have to look at employee satisfaction and engagement for a really unpopular change and accept that a 65 percent engagement rate is as good as it gets.

One also has to look at how success is defined in order to see what the organization has accomplished. Is the change a smaller process-related one that impacts only three to four employees and has a discrete, short-term beginning and end? Or is it a massive change with underlying cultural issues that impact all of the staff members in one or more departments? In the latter case, one may have to break the change up into smaller chunks where one can celebrate smaller milestones.

One has to consider these factors in determining how successful a change was. Another key issue to explore in determining whether the change was successful and proceeded well is whether it accomplished the original purpose of the change. Ultimately, one asks the question, did it result in the needed cultural change? Has it led to faster processing tasks or a more harmonious work environment? Finally, does it need to be adjusted or improved upon?

It is through the evaluation process, which will be discussed more in chapter 8, that managers can discover if the change implementation process was successful and subsequently whether they were effective as change leaders. This discovery is usually achieved by collecting data in the areas of change. Some measures could include less staff to run a more efficient process, increased productivity, and increased usage as an equivalent to sales in the commercial arena. It can also be important to assess employee resilience in the aftermath of the change and how one is regarded as a leader. Despite the importance of the evaluation process, very few managers complete this final change stage. Without performing the evaluation process, managers can reach the conclusion that they led a successful change process, when in fact this was not the case.

KEYS TO SUCCESS

In summarizing the key elements of leading the actual implementation of a change, there are several important roles for the change leader.

- Staying focused on leadership and guiding employee growth through the process
- Supporting empowerment through the delegation of implementation details
- Finding a balance between paying attention to the important minutiae and progressing toward the big-picture result
- Being flexible in developing situational solutions on the fly
- Engaging with all levels of the organization on both the big-picture changes and minutiae as appropriate
- Communicating, communicating, and more communicating . . . which is a dialogue process that includes listening and responding to others' comments

THINKING EXERCISES

1. You have proposed a change in workflow priorities. Four impacted staff members seem comfortable with the change. However, two other staff members are opposed to it. After some discussion where the opposing staff members do not speak up much, you authorize the change to take place. However, one of the opposing staff members keeps bringing the

issue up in meetings, as if it were still an open discussion topic, and the other staff member simply seems to be ignoring the new priorities and doing his work the same way as before the change was implemented. How do you engage with the two individuals in order to move forward the changed priorities?

Subsequently as you are talking to them, one of the individuals brings up as a reason for not supporting the change the fact that you had overlooked an aspect of the new priorities that might put it in conflict with institution fund management and compliance rules. What do you do now?

2. Suppose you are planning to rearrange the work space for more efficient tracking and handling of library materials through the workflow. What parts of the implementation offer opportunities for employee empowerment and bringing them into the decision-making process in an active way?

3. You have realized that in planning a change involving your own staff, you did not include a key stakeholder from another unit in the implementation communications. The implementation is approximately 40 percent completed, and this person has come to you upset at being "the last to know." What do you say and do to reestablish the relationship with the individual and incorporate some of the employee's legitimate concerns and feedback into the implementation process?

4. You have spent the summer leading a change team through the process of planning and implementing a new workflow for putting materials into the course reserve system more efficiently. A month into the fall academic term, you get a complaint from a course instructor about how long it is taking to process course reserves materials. You check with the unit and discover that the more efficient workflow never "happened" and staff are still doing it the "old" way. In response to basic inquiries, you get responses indicating uncertainty and disconnects about what the final version of the new workflow looked like and when it was supposed to "start" because some employees were on vacation in July and August. What do you do now?

5. As you went through these exercises, what were your own emotions in picturing yourself in these situations, and how could your reaction to

those emotions lead to the implementation process faltering or to getting it reengaged and moving along?

NOTES

1. Davis M. Woodruff, "How to Effectively Manage Change," *Hydrocarbon Processing* 75, no. 1 (1996): 145.
2. Robert A. Paton and James McCalman, *Change Management: A Guide to Effective Implementation*, 3rd ed. (Los Angeles: Sage, 2008), 144.
3. Carol Hansen Montgomery and JoAnne L. Sparks, "The Transition to an Electronic Journal Collection: Managing the Organizational Changes," *Serials Review* 26, no. 3 (2000): 4–18.
4. Colin Carnall, *The Change Management Toolkit* (London: Thomson, 2003), 105.
5. D. Brian Harrison and Maurice D. Pratt, "A Methodology for Reengineering Businesses," *Strategic Leadership* 21, no. 2 (1993): 6–11.
6. Robert N. Lussier and Christopher F. Achua, *Leadership: Theory, Application, Skill Development*, 4th ed. (Mason, OH: Thomson/South-Wester, 2009).
7. Woodruff, "How to Effectively Manage Change," 143–48.
8. Jean M. Bartunek and others, "Managers and Project Leaders: Conducting Their Own Action Research Interventions," in *Handbook of Organizational Consultation*, 2nd ed., ed. Robert T. Golembiewski (New York: Marcel Dekker, 2000), 59–70.
9. Carolyn A. Gallagher and others, "Implementing Organizational Change," in *Implementing Organizational Interventions: Steps, Processes, and Best Practices*, ed. Jerry W. Hedge and Elaine D. Pulakos (San Francisco: Jossey-Bass, 2002), 12.
10. Ibid., 21.
11. Dianne R. Stober, "Making It Stick: Coaching as a Tool for Organizational Change," *Coaching: An International Journal of Theory, Research and Practice* 1, no. 1 (2008): 71–80.
12. Gallagher, "Implementing Organizational Change," 25.
13. Gordon L. Lippitt and others, *Implementing Organizational Change: A Practical Guide to Managing Change Efforts* (San Francisco: Jossey-Bass, 1985), 111.
14. Jerry W. Hedge and Elaine D. Pulakos, "Grappling with Implementation: Some Preliminary Thoughts and Relevant Research," in *Implementing Organizational Interventions: Steps, Processes, and Best Practices*, ed. Jerry W. Hedge and Elaine D. Pulakos (San Francisco: Jossey-Bass, 2002), 1–11.
15. Gallagher, "Implementing Organizational Change," 26.
16. Bert Spector, *Implementing Organizational Change: Theory and Practice* (New Jersey: Prentice Hall, 2007), 195.
17. Ibid.
18. Bill Leban and Romuald Stone, *Managing Organizational Change*, 2nd ed. (New Jersey: John Wiley, 2008), 135.
19. Ibid.
20. Thomas R. Haevey, *Checklist for Change: A Pragmatic Approach to Creating and Controlling Change*, 2nd ed. (Lancaster, PA: Technomic, 1995), 84.

21. Leban and Stone, *Managing Organizational Change*, 136.
22. Ibid.
23. Ibid., 135–36.
24. Tupper Cawsey and Gene Deszca, *Toolkit for Organizational Change* (Los Angeles: Sage, 2007), 283.
25. Susan Carol Curzon, *Managing Change: A How-to-Do-It Manual for Librarians*, rev. ed. (London: Facet, 2006), 83.
26. Spector, *Implementing Organizational Change*, 171.
27. Ibid., 172.
28. General (Ret.) Colin Powell, 2nd Brigade Combat Team of the 28th Infantry Division, *Iron Soldier Newsletter*, February 15, 2006.
29. Curzon, *Managing Change*, 84.
30. Sandra Nelson, *Strategic Planning for Results* (Chicago: American Library Association, 2008), 224–25.
31. Ibid., 225.

CHAPTER 6

ENVIRONMENTAL FACTORS IMPACTING SUCCESS

Character is not made in a crisis, it is only exhibited.

—Robert Freeman

AS MUCH AS a leader tries to plan and engage with the stakeholders on an organizational change and incorporate their suggestions, there are always going to be issues beyond one's control that impact the project and stakeholder participation, which is why it is important to remain flexible. These issues can come from a variety of sources. In some cases, during the diagnostics phase of implementation, these may be predicted based on larger organizational constraints.[1] In other cases, they may be unexpected and catch everyone off guard. Nelson believes this is why some change leaders have difficulty putting their strategic plan into reality, that the problems become more complex during implementation than the initial issues the team faced during the planning process.[2] The impact of these issues can vary widely. Even as one may not be able to do anything about the issue itself, change leaders can exert some control on the response based on the manner in which they communicate the event or issue and address its impact. This is done so that the change leaders can gather additional feedback on the employees' attitudes toward the new organizational problem and to "challenge any misconceptions, and to clarify new organizational roles, structures and systems."[3] The most effective change leaders are those who can maintain a balance of realistic hope and idealism even when sharing bad news. This does not mean one is superficially positive or oblivious to concerns, but that one takes a calming attitude that addresses the problem as a challenge that can be overcome or worked around.

According to Nelson, there are four reasons why some libraries have trouble meeting their implementation goals. The first is that the library administration did not supply the resources required to completely implement the activities that were needed to maintain the change. The second is that activities chosen to support the change were not as successful as the library administration expected them to be. The third is that the library administration did not carry forward sufficient activities to attain the implementation goal. The fourth is that the library administration positioned the implementation goals too high.[4]

Employees often feel let down and begin to stress about their position within the library when it becomes clear that the reality will not live up to the vision that everyone had bought into. They feel like they have failed in some way to achieve the goal they had bought into. One of the drawbacks of having effectively engaged with staff during the development, planning, and implementation stages is that they may have bought into the change with a near-utopian vision of success. When utopia fails or, worse, begins to more clearly resemble the mundane world, there can be a backlash reaction of emotional frustration and disillusionment. Brunstein believes that failure normally induces employees to develop a negative attitude that will decrease the chance that they will buy into future organizational initiatives.[5] Adding to this problem, failure can lead employees to feel humiliated and belittled by having believed in the change so fully, which in turn hinders their future performance.

There are several techniques to avoid this. Obviously the first technique is to try and anticipate as many delays or disruptions as possible and publicly factor them into the implementation plan timeline. Additionally, one should try to balance enthusiastic engagement and overly optimistic idealism by encouraging some individuals to take the role of being the voice of reason to keep the change grounded in reality from the start and to discourage the perception that one will achieve library nirvana or perfection with the change. Alternately, if the idealism has taken on a life of its own, focus on providing employees with reassurance that their world will not end and that the change will still be a positive one even if it does not achieve as much or happen as quickly and smoothly as they had hoped. In addition, don't ignore the small signs of possible problems. Paraskevas believes that to be an effective manager you must prepare for a crisis even if that crisis might never occur.[6] For example, if a reporter calls asking unexpected or confusing questions about something operational, this could be a clue to you that there is a problem. The important point to remember is: "Failure to address key aspects of the change process can either add years to, or even prevent, achieving successful implementation."[7]

ANTICIPATED DELAYS

Sometimes an experienced, engaged manager or change leader will be able to antici-pate some of the specific problems that are likely to come up once the implementa-tion of a change begins. Ruff and Aziz believe that "risk auditing" can also help the manager anticipate a possible crisis.[8] A risk audit requires that the key team members of each department participate in a regular examination of all their activities to see how they could be affected by a crisis. These come from institutional and personal knowledge, such as knowing that facilities services *always* underestimates the amount of time or resources needed for renovations. They can also come from having super-visory experience as a change leader and recognizing that particular employees tend to hit a wall and begin looking for guidance and reassurance at a certain point of the implementation process when they better understand the change. It can also come from having been through changes and knowing that when individuals are enthusiastic about a change, they do not want to be thinking about the negative realities and effects that could hold up the change. When this occurs coaching can play an important role in helping the employees advance and learn more about the implementation of the change.[9] However, all of these examples can take time.[10] In these cases, one needs to factor in some undefined slippage time or simply insert "just-in-case," "catch-up," or "pause and reassess" windows in the implementation plan without getting into a debate about whether one is being an optimist or pessimist about the change itself.

One good rule of thumb when dealing with a change that involves physical space is to increase one's slippage window for each independent factor in the change. For example, if one is renovating an office area and the plan calls for facilities services to install new carpet and paint before constructing and installing new furniture, it is important to realize that there are several invisible opportunities for environmental factors to delay the change. The first is the delivery of the paint and carpet; then there is the delivery of the furniture; finally, there is the factor of something being delivered wrong, either in quantity or condition, and having to be rushed redelivered. Suppose one is rewiring an area for more computers; it will be important to allow extra time for the postinstallation inspection to find something that needs to be addressed, despite reassurances to the contrary from the contractor who guarantees it will be done per-fectly the first time. Ultimately, in most library projects one has to accept that even though the project may be your number one priority with a direct impact on library users, the various contractors that one is dealing with may not see the project the same way. For example, in an academic environment, facilities services may have classroom and dorm projects as a higher priority than other services or office spaces during summer terms or interim periods because of their high occupancy during the regular academic terms. In this environment, one would not want to schedule a renovation on a tight summer timeline that relies on facilities services.

When dealing with staff and changing workflows or organizational structures, the slippage time is needed to allow people to go through the emotional process of accepting the change that was discussed in chapter 2. There are additional factors that can introduce delays as well. For example, changes in organizational reporting lines are all about breaking up and building new professional and personal relationships, which does not happen overnight, and those leaders who believe that it can are doomed to fail. This can be particularly difficult if there is grapevine baggage about a particular supervisor or employee that must be overcome in building the relationship. Individuals must learn each other's communication style and expectations, another experiential component that is based on opportunities for interactions over a period of time. It is also important to keep in mind that even with well-structured on-the-job training, employees do not learn new procedures or skills instantaneously, and a window of time must be allowed for the training to be put into practice and absorbed as employees go through a settling-in stage. What is most curious is that many staff immersed in the process of change often overlook these lag times because of their commitment or enthusiasm for the change. When individuals do mention these types of concerns, there may be peer pressure suggesting that the individual is against the change. Therefore, it is part of the change leader's responsibility to verify that these adjustment periods are factored into the change plan. There are also human resources process windows if the change requires hiring new temporary or permanent employees. Even in a downturned economy with large hiring pools, hiring is not necessarily a fast process. One may encounter delays because one is working with a lot of different schedules in setting up interviews and checking references. One final delay that is often overlooked by change leaders and stakeholders is allowing for the time to communicate details and decisions about the change to the stakeholders appropriately. In a major reorganization, it is a better approach to meet with key individuals in addition to the subsequent public announcement to all. For a larger department with employees working different shifts this might take several days, yet is often overlooked as part of the timeline in the initial planning process.

As a change leader, one has two primary responsibilities related to addressing anticipated delays. The first is to deliberately avoid the overenthusiastic idealism that encourages tight timelines with everything going smoothly. Laszlo and Laugel call this developing ambitions that are greater than means.[11] The reality of any major change is that one will encounter delays and that as more people are involved in the change, individual parts will take longer to accomplish. By anticipating these ahead of time, one is not being negative. Instead one will be able to say quite honestly that the project is still on schedule when announcing that the carpet installation has been delayed because the work crew was diverted to work on a dorm during the December holiday break. It also means one can emphasize patience when individuals struggle to learn new skills or develop effective interactions with individuals they have not worked closely with in the past. This leads to a second key responsibility as a change leader: minimizing organizational overreaction to a delay by using effective communication techniques that reduce the crisis response and refocus on the overall goal. Ruff and Aziz point out that in an attempt to stop a crisis from developing some organizations react excessively and make a problem worse than it initially was.[12] This will be reviewed in the sections on dealing with unexpected delays, but is also an important part of delays related to issues that could be anticipated. It only increases stakeholder confidence in you as a leader to hear calmly that you had considered the possibility of this happening and taken it into account when setting project milestones or adjusting an original plan.

UNEXPECTED DELAYS

In spite of one's best efforts at anticipating what might go awry when leading a major change initiative, one does not have perfect foresight, and there will be issues within any major change initiative that one could not have been expected to anticipate which can create a crisis situation within the organization. This is partly because directly or indirectly, change involves people and communications between individuals. People are complex entities with a high degree of unpredictability because individuals respond to any situation through their own filters and perspectives. Similarly, communication is one of the most challenging aspects of people working together. It is amazing how individuals can leave a meeting with a totally different understanding of what is going to happen next and who is responsible for which action item, particularly in more complicated change initiatives. Paton and McCalman stress that "if organizations do not manage their communications, others will. The media, the unions, the 'rumour mill' and competitors are only too willing to assist the 'silent' corporation in its time of need."[13]

However, even though it ultimately comes down to the people involved in the change as the common denominator, environmental factors can be a trigger for different change participants or stakeholders to react in a way that leads to unanticipated delays. These unexpected delays tend to fall into several major categories: budget, institutional bureaucracy, staff turnover, weather, and personalities. So even as one cannot anticipate the details of the delay, as a change leader one can be prepared for a delay of this type and watch for warning signs of a problem and communicate appropriately. In today's ever-changing society, crisis management studies have become increasingly important when discussing organizational change.[14] Despite the experienced leader's best attempt at foreseeing and strategically planning for delay, organizational planning and implementation plans can be wiped away in one moment by an unforeseen organizational crisis and can become the ultimate test of a leader.

BUDGET CONCERNS

If the 1990s were a period of growth for many libraries, the first decade of the twenty-first century was one of cautious regrouping that ended with outright budget angst. The financial issues that led to crashing investments did not spare libraries and prompted the initiation of new changes and disrupted in-progress changes. Unfortunately, one cannot always predict when a budget crisis can strike, and since many large-scale projects may have multiyear timelines, one may find oneself suddenly applying crisis management skills in dealing with budget issues. Even beyond organizational budget crises, one can also be hit by project costs that have been initially underestimated or one may encounter unexpected cost overruns.

No matter what part of the country one is in, space renovations have gotten expensive. With the increased attention to environmental factors and technology needs, putting up or taking down walls has become more complex. Following the 2005 hurricane season with Hurricane Katrina hitting New Orleans and Hurricane Rita hitting nearby Texas, some residential and commercial construction materials were in short supply in the southern United States and more expensive when one could get them. This resulted in higher rates for supplies and installers that would not have been in an original budget estimate. Renovations may also have hidden costs that do not get revealed until the demolition stage of the project. One example of this would be the installation of a sprinkler system to bring an older building up to public safety codes. As the ceiling grid is removed, the foreman discovers that some beams are covered with asbestos, a material that is now identified as hazardous and requires a specialized encapsulation and/or removal process. One can also find asbestos and other hazardous materials such as lead or arsenic embedded in tiles, paints, and adhesives used between the 1920s and 1960s. So long as they are not disturbed they are not a health hazard, but when it comes to removal it is a different story. The result of this is that the original cost estimates go up and project timelines get extended dramatically. For library employees who are already pushed out of their comfort zone in preparing for the change as it was initially planned, these sorts of events can seriously undermine their confidence in the success of the project and increase their level of stress. According to Lewis, the foundation for the basic building blocks of stress is determined by three factors: (1) how important the event is to the employee, (2) lack of clarity about the outcome of the event, and (3) the time factor involved.[15] All of these can come into play during the change process when faced with delays. However, stress can be decreased by communicating to your employees information about the crisis.

In some cases, a budgetary development may require one to make minor or major adjustments to the change implementation. Minor adjustments can be more easily absorbed, with the key leadership factor being to keep everyone informed. No employees want to feel they have been made to look stupid or out of touch in front of their peers or library users by not having the most up-to-date information on the status of a project. For major adjustments where one may have to scale back the change or dramatically change a timeline or not be able to fill positions as expected, the disruption can have a much bigger impact on organizational morale. In this case, leaders may have to step back and actually rebuild buy-in for a revised version of the plan in order to reinforce that the change is still moving in the right direction, even as the optimal model cannot be accomplished at this time. A consistent theme throughout this book is that the leader should work to emulate a reliable, confident demeanor that, even as it respects that there are budget issues, does not promote a panic, pullback response. Ruff and Aziz state that managers must let their employees know that they are working on the crisis because that tells the employees that their manager is handling the problem.[16] Budget concerns can create a fear reaction in many employees: am I going to be laid off, is my salary that barely pays the bills going to be cut, is my workload going to increase multifold as vacated positions cannot be refilled, and so on? This leads to a tendency to think and overreact as if the whole world is failing, with worst-case scenarios prevailing. Effective change leaders will not make false promises but will provide updates on a regular basis and present a calming public face. Once stakeholders have gotten past the initial shock reaction and been reassured that the world is not ending, leaders can reengage with them on the substantive adjustments to the plan.

When dealing with budget factors impacting change, the leader's role as provider of accurate and timely information is critical. With these sorts of emotional responses, saying one does not have any details or answers yet but that they will be shared as soon as they are available is also important. This is something that many leaders may forget as they get caught up in the actual management of the budget problem. But this will be when it is most important to keep the lines of communication open. It is also where one may get some of the best ideas for coping with the budgetary shortfall. Few of us go into librarianship for the money or to get rich. That said, professional librarians and administrators will tend to earn the higher of the salaries in the organization and may have moved beyond the point of needing to exercise small economies to pay the bills or make ends meet. However, for many of the staff, this is their normal mode of operation, and appealing to them to provide ideas on how to scale back a change initiative in response to temporary budget shortfalls may introduce many ideas that change leaders or managers never would have considered on their own. One of the worst responses a change leader can make is to deliver an announcement with incorrect information or make an announcement with the details of the budget at the same time that one announces the decision of how the library will be making the cut or will modify the change initiative.

INSTITUTIONAL BUREAUCRACY

Another area of unanticipated delays that leaders and managers can encounter when implementing changes are those that are caused by the multitude of rules and policies and procedures dictated from an organizational level. Implementing change is one of those situations when being small and independent can be a definite advantage. In truth, many innovative developments in librarianship come out of smaller academic institutions with less than a few thousand students because one has the personal relationships established to try innovative approaches without running afoul of the bureaucracy of the larger Carnegie I research institutions with tens of thousands of students. Managers and supervisors encounter and learn to work with and around the routine institutional bureaucracy on a daily basis. But for a developing leader of a change project or even an experienced manager encountering a new aspect of institutional bureaucracy, it can be frustrating, confusing, and difficult to incorporate into a project schedule. If this type of crisis does occur, it is critical for the manager to continue projecting a serious but generally positive outlook for employees about the change. The last thing an organization needs is a manager who is upsetting staff with doomsday prophecies. It is important not to forget about your staff and continue communicating to them what is happening. Sometimes the result of a bureaucratic crisis may require one to actually shorten the timeline for a milestone. Staff members need to know why the implementation timeline was pushed up so they don't resent a possible increase in workload because the implementation timeline got pushed up.[17]

Institutional bureaucracy permeates most aspects of operations at medium to large colleges and universities or large public library systems. When embarking on a major renovation or reorganization, one is going to encounter a host of offices that must be consulted or must sign off on one's plans, processes, or decisions. Imagine how senseless and frustrating it can be to front-line staff members to feel that their excellent suggestion about moveable furnishings cannot be implemented because the supplier is not an approved vendor. Or to get past supplier issues and then encounter institutional safety reprimands because the moveable furniture is left blocking access to the mechanical rooms or evacuation corridors that are so critical in large multistory buildings. Change leaders must develop skills to present the bureaucratic impediments to the change in a matter-of-fact way that explains the underlying reasons for the policy without encouraging staff to "blame" the other parts of the institution.

One area where change leaders will often run into significant institutional bureaucracy delays are matters involving personnel resources. These can vary and may include factors such as the normal review process when one is changing a position's responsibilities for verification of classification appropriateness, delays in creating or filling new positions, or even having to deal with the investigation of a grievance filed by an employee who is having a particularly difficult time adjusting to the changing expectations. The first two examples are ones that can reasonably be anticipated and included to some degree in the original timeline. The third example is not totally predictable in the sense that managers might not know when a particular employee reaches a personal tipping point that would launch a grievance process. However, if a leader knows that a large number of employees are going to be pushed significantly outside of their comfort zones and will be expected to change their job responsibilities or learn new skills and tools, then it is realistic to expect that questions will get raised at a higher level, and allowing time for the investigation and resolution is advisable. One does not have to put it on the plan explicitly as "disgruntled employee delays," but one can use more euphemistic phrasing such as "human resources review process" or "organizational inspections/approvals." This protects the employee privacy legalities but keeps the potential impact on the change initiative from being an overlooked delay.

As one is incorporating some organizational delays into one's change plan it is important to get realistic estimates. Even if one is not trying to negotiate a rush or expedited treatment, which is discussed in more detail shortly, it is helpful to open communications with third parties sooner rather than later. As an example, suppose under normal conditions it takes human resources officers three business days to review and approve a revised position responsibilities statement. If you know that a proposed reorganization will require the review of twenty-five revised position descriptions at once, then it is best to get an estimate from the reviewing office to find out when is the best time to submit the revisions and how long to allow for their review. It is important to recognize that even having done the legwork to estimate the time, there is no guarantee that the estimate will still be valid when one has reached that part of the plan. Suppose even as you are sending in your twenty-five new position descriptions, two other departments elsewhere in the institution were also doing a major reorganization. Now instead of having to work in twenty-five extra position description reviews, the human resources officers are trying to juggle seventy-five position reviews. As an alternate scenario, suppose that about the time you are submitting your twenty-five positions for review, the institutional administration determines there is a need for a human resources audit. Staff may be immediately diverted from the "routine" review of position descriptions to pull files together for auditors on the past year's hiring or timekeeping processes. The key is to not have scheduled this part of the project in a way that it is a critical path milestone, where a delay will stall the entire implementation. In this way, one can keep morale up and retain forward progress by continuing with other parts of the implementation plan while the bureaucratic components work to their own schedule.

As a change leader one will need to consider where one has created allies or built equity to push past the bureaucratic delays, and one will also need to decide which issues are worth fighting. Opening dialogue early about what one's institutional needs is an excellent start. In doing so, one gets a verbal commitment from the other party and avoids the perception of being an overly demanding, uncommunicative individual. One cannot ask for every personnel decision involving a change initiative to be a crisis. If you follow this model of always being the squeaky wheel pushing for fast resolution outside of the normal process, you will become the manager that no one else wants to deal with and your requests will be deliberately put at the bottom of the stack. As recommended previously, if one has built bureaucratic delays into the original timeline and set them parallel to other implementation activities, one will not have to address the situation as a problem. It also better positions one to enter a priority negotiation or request that a process be expedited if a real problem or delay does develop.

STAFF TURNOVER

Related to the previous areas of institutional bureaucracy and budget issues, another environmental factor that can impact a change initiative in several different ways is staff turnover. Organizations encounter significant costs when they face staff turnovers. Not only do they encounter costs related to recruitment and training, but also indirect costs of a loss of staff morale and organizational memory.[18] Unfortunately, staff turnover during an organizational change is often only minimally predictable, and according to Morrell and others, there is a gap in the existing literature that explores the link between organizational change and staff turnover.[19] If a long-term employee who is well within the age and seniority to take full retirement benefits has spoken publicly about being unhappy with proposed changes and has mentioned retiring, then one may not be too surprised when it actually happens. However, there are many staff and librarians who, for a variety of personal reasons, do not talk about leaving until the day they submit their resignation. When it occurs during a change initiative, this can leave staff members to start pumping the grapevine with their view of why a person left. Depending on who leaves, staff turnover can have a significant impact on the implementation of a change. At the simplest level of losing a front-line employee, you have the disruption of having to sidetrack resources and engagement on the change initiative in order to work on hiring a replacement and training that person. Alternately, if you are on the cusp of implementing the final stages of the change, it may be necessary to wait to fill the vacancy until the new structure or initiatives are in place. In this case, one must redistribute the critical workload pieces to others, even while they are stressed about the other changes taking place. This can be very difficult and requires an empathic response to the individual one is asking to effectively overload in the short term. If the person who leaves had a clear role in the change implementation, then it is necessary to reapportion the individual's responsibilities to others. Change implementation will fail if staff members are asked to perform new activities for an extended period of time while being fully occupied with their current job responsibilities.[20] Depending on what they are already taking on related to the operational change, there may be a sense of reluctance to take on more. This is particularly problematic if the change initiative requires staff to learn new skills or routines. In some cases, turnover will lead to the loss of a significant amount of process knowledge. While this is never a good thing in the best of times, when one is leading a change initiative it can lead to making bad operational decisions at a critical time. This may require you to refocus and immerse yourself in the operational details to make sure as much thought is given and input sought on the operational decisions as possible in order to avoid the disintegration and eventual breakdown of the change. Although the potential that a change will fall apart is ever present, it is more likely to occur during a time of difficulty. Curzon believes that the key to stopping the change from going off course is by recognizing the problems early in order to manage the change breakdown and steer the team back on course.[21]

Up to this point we have explored the logistical aspects of dealing with staff turnover in the middle of implementing change. There is also an emotional component that change leaders will need to be aware of and in some cases take an intervention role in addressing. If the person who has left was a perpetual naysayer, was actively against the change initiative, or had convinced everyone that they could not adapt, there may be a quiet sigh of relief that the person is gone. However, one should not relax too quickly. As a leader, one may have to do damage control to an organizational perception that the individual was encouraged to leave or was no longer appreciated by the administration. For those who are struggling with buying into the change or nervous about the impact it will have on their responsibilities, a peer's departure can undermine their own confidence at being able to adapt or their confidence in the success of the change, and can be seen as the ultimate step in undermining an organizational change. It will be important to reassure them that their situation is different from the person who left, even while one is maintaining professional confidentiality on the departed employee. In truth, this creates an opportunity for a leader to deliberately hire a candidate who will be engaged and supportive of the postchange model. From the opposite perspective, if the person who has left was a grassroots leader in building enthusiasm for the change, then the sense of loss in enthusiasm and support for getting through the change may temporarily undermine forward progress of the change. It will be your responsibility as a change leader to fill the gap left by the person's departure. One does so by reengaging on the molecular level with what people are going through in implementing the change and grow someone else into a grassroots leader role. It will also require offering public reassurance that the change can still be successful even without the absent employee.

Another difficulty of dealing with turnover during the implementation of a change initiative is when a departure is accompanied by an institutional hiring freeze. In this case, one may have to actually reevaluate the planned change and question whether adjustments need to be made in the context of the diminished staffing support. The response will depend on the criticality of the individual's role in implementing the change. If the individual was a major participant in the change, it may be necessary to reestablish confidence that the change can still be implemented, even as one may have to consider scaling back the scope of the project or extending the timeline. In this situation, it will be critical to use the techniques discussed in earlier chapters to reengage with stakeholders and rebuild confidence in the success of the change initiative. If one is actually dealing with a significant reduction in force or extended hiring freeze, then it may be necessary to hold off starting the actual implementation until its feasibility can be reaffirmed. If the implementation has already begun and one is past a point of no return, then getting buy-in from the other stakeholders impacted by the plan to strategize priorities is essential.

There is another aspect of turnover that is worth mentioning as well. This is when the person who has left is an administrator or manager responsible for initiating and leading the change. In some cases, delays in or failure of the change initiative may be unavoidable if buy-in has not been accomplished and there is still major resistance to the change at the time of the person's departure. Similarly, if the individual has held the oversight and implementation of the change close, delays may come as others try to figure out what was going on. However, if the change implementation plan has been communicated and managed effectively, then it will be easier to point out that the project is bigger than that one person and to continue progress with only a minor hiccup as the individual's responsibilities are redistributed and others step into the leadership role.

WEATHER

Another factor that can be impossible to predict but can wreak havoc on a change initiative is weather. This can be local weather that delays a building construction project or pouring concrete for a new patio, or it can be weather elsewhere in the nation or world. Consider, for example, that in winter 2010 many states experienced record-setting snowfalls. Suppose one of those snowfalls occurred in the state where the new library furnishings were being manufactured and shipped from. Imagine your horror at watching the news and hear them talking about how the flat roof of the manufacturer's warehouse has caved in from the weight of the snow. This is followed the next day by a call from the manufacturer explaining that your furniture shipment is under that snow and will be delayed by six to eight months. Some might consider this example overly dramatic, yet it perfectly illustrates the total lack of control one has in planning for or affecting some events relating to a change implementation. The only option one has is to accept that which cannot be changed and gauge how to respond to it in a way that does not undermine the entire project and confidence in it.

In this example, it might be prudent to exercise an escape clause from the first vendor and look for a different vendor that could deliver earlier. Alternately, one could accept that for a few months one will have beautiful walls and finishes on built-ins, but old, mismatched stained chairs and tables. It partly depends on what the impact of the delayed component is on the project as a whole and which subsequent milestones are impacted. Using the snowbound furniture example, suppose the furniture was the last item for completion and a grand opening extravaganza of the new space was planned for the month following the furniture delivery. In this situation, one can either look for alternate furniture options that will still meet the deadline or move the grand opening extravaganza. Part of the decision process will be assessing how locked-in the organization is for the grand opening. Has it been widely announced? Are special guests (donors, institutional dignitaries, etc.) already committed with extensive travel plans made? Will one lose money exercising change clauses for caterers? Alternately, what would be the costs of expediting furniture from another vendor? It is also important not to forget the role of negotiation. Suppose you went back to the original snowbound supplier and asked if they could get you a partial order from their other warehouses by the time of the grand opening that you could scatter around the space to give a sense of how the seating will be configured. In this case, it can appear you needed to remove some furniture arrangements to make room for the special guests but still provide a sense of the finished space for the event.

Dealing with unanticipated weather-related delays during a change initiative may closely resemble crisis management, where one can only do so much to actually control the details of the situation but must apply extensive focus and energies to the follow-up recovery process. In this case, one may not have time to carry out a fully engaged dialogue with everyone involved in the change. Rather, one should send out brief updates or news releases so that stakeholders are aware of what is going on, and one should bring together a core action group to consider the impact of the delay, brainstorm possible responses, and make a decision on what to do next. It is optimal, but not always possible, to have some representation from major stakeholder areas on the decision group. Then as soon as some decisions are reached, one should communicate with the stakeholders directly through e-mail, an intranet site, or a called meeting to update them about what is going on. Along with the actual decisions and the impact they will have on the change implementation, this communication should include the context of what happened to trigger the crisis and the decision methodology that was used to cope with it. It is important to share why there was a need for an urgent response to avoid staff feeling that they were not engaged on a critical aspect of the project. It is also valuable to be able to say one has already considered a variety of ideas that the stakeholders might bring forward and why the ideas were not adopted as part of the change.

PERSONALITIES

One of the last areas of unanticipated delays one may encounter in trying to lead the change implementation is the least predictable and can have the potential to completely undermine a change initiative. Titled "Personalities," this section actually deals with the personal and emotional response of change stakeholders and observers that may develop as the change goes through the implementation process. There has been considerable research about how employees' feelings and perceptions advance as the organizational change process develops.[22] Earlier parts of this book emphasized the importance of developing shared vision and understanding of the change on the part of the stakeholders as well as the importance of not fostering too much idealistic optimism. It also talked about the role of emotions in accepting the ideas behind the change. Once the change implementation actually starts, emotions can still play a major role in the success of the change.

Change creates a stressful environment.[23] Even those employees who are in favor of the change are experiencing stress as their work environment is changing. For those that are less enthusiastic about the change, the stress is heightened with over-tones of uncertainty about their future success. During such a period, it is too easy for the small personality conflicts that employees would normally ignore or brush off to become major irritants that undermine cooperation and collegiality. Suppose a member of the team has a pattern behavior of ending every comment in a meeting with the self-deprecating phrase "of course you wouldn't understand my perspective." With staff members already in a stressed state from having their world turned upside down by the change, what was a tolerated idiosyncrasy on the part of individuals that everyone ignored becomes a personalized attack from individuals suggesting people do not want to listen and cooperate with them. Individuals start getting defensive and emotions begin to rule every interaction. The next thing a manager knows is that staff members are at the office door making complaints about the coworker. Another varia-tion can occur when staff members who are less enthusiastic about a change see peer staff members who are approaching a change initiative in a positive and enthusiastic way and appearing to be more at peace and successful. Rather than look to their own attitude about the change as a source of their personal frustration or unhappiness, instead these individuals think they are missing out on some kind of extra support or favoritism that the happier employee is getting. The next thing the manager knows is that a report has been filed with human resources that the employee against the change is being treated unfairly or discriminated against.

While a change leader cannot delay the implementation of a change while everyone becomes happy and comfortable together with every aspect of the change, one can work with employees to encourage them to keep some perspective and compartmental-ize their responses to their peers. This may mean creating a cooling-off period where a third party or the manager is a go-between. It can also be useful to point out that the irritating behavior is not new, as is often the case. Rather, it is the complaining indi-vidual's response to the behavior that has moved the perception of the behavior from the mildly tedious or predictable category to the bothersome or irritating perspective. Similarly, it may be necessary to point out to an individual their own responsibility in contributing to their level of professional satisfaction and explicitly explain that it is not about others but more about themselves. While managers and change leaders may refer employees that are struggling with a change environment to an institution's employee assistance program, it is important to realize that often programs are also available to change leaders to help them understand how to mediate conflict and motivate employees more effectively. Managers who expect to find themselves in change leadership roles should watch for appropriate self-development opportunities to develop their leadership skills in conflict resolution.

Finally, one should keep in mind as one is developing the change implementation schedule whether there are external events that will contribute to a more highly stressed response from individuals going through some type of organizational change. It is best if one can work the schedule around the additional stressor event. However, if it is simply not possible, then one should focus on being prepared for a heightened level of stress and expect to spend more time smoothing over conflict and de-escalating reactions. These events can be work or nonwork related. An example of a work-related higher stress period is that of annual evaluations. However, an individual's work stress tolerance can also be impacted by nonwork events such as major holidays with significant family demands. Separate from the weather logistical issues discussed earlier is the issue of how weather can impact individuals working together in the final implementation stages of a change. Suppose one is at a library where the "severe" or most stressful period of the year is winter with heavy snowfalls requiring cleanup and extra care in traveling. People may be kept inside and closer together because it is too cold to get out for casual exercise. As a related issue, seasonal affective disorder is a documented condition that can impact one's sense of emotional well-being and affect one's motivation.[24] Similarly, in southern climates, the period from late July to mid-September when the heat is most intense and seems to never end can lead to short tempers. Combining the peak stress of a change implementation with a period where individuals cannot get outside or away from others easily means that one may end up spending more time fostering patience and reconciliations. The emphasis in all of these situations is recognizing the source of the conflict and not letting it escalate in a way that undermines the overall success of the change initiative.

KEYS TO SUCCESS

In summarizing the key aspects of dealing with environmental factors that can undermine change implementation, there are several approaches to keep in mind.

- Try to anticipate implementation detours and holdups as much as possible and factor them into the timeline. A little pessimism is a good thing, and in many cases if the estimate seems too optimistic, then it probably is.
- Build equity with contractors and other institutional stakeholders by giving them the option and consideration of being able to plan around each other's needs.
- Do not panic at the unexpected and maintain a calm, confident public demeanor. Expressing concern is appropriate and can validate one's sincerity, but keep the shock and hysteria behind closed doors.
- Be willing to recognize when a situation has gone very bad and that one is going to have to revise one's expectations for the change.
- Stay encouraging about buy-in, even as the vision may have to be revised or modified.
- Keep stakeholders informed on developing interruptions, adjustments, negotiations, and compromises.
- Get refresher conflict management or mediator training.

THINKING EXERCISES

1. Suppose you were implementing a change impacting workflows for the staff in your unit that will require staff to use technology tools more. Who would you anticipate would have the most difficulty learning the new technology skills? How would you address this individual's concerns or reactions in the context of the entire change?

2. You are coordinating the creation of an outdoor patio space for library users. Over a period of one month, concrete will be poured for pathways and seating pads, beds will be prepared and shrubs and flowers planted, and heavy-duty outdoor tables and chairs installed (bolted down). Given your current location and usage patterns, what time of year is the best time to do this project and why?

   How would you modify your plans if you learned the only time the job could be done was when there would likely be some delays due to unstable weather patterns?

3. You have developed the following basic project outline for converting the 250,000-volume collection of a branch library from bar codes to RFID tags. What would the timeline look like at your institution to

carry out this project? Where would you need to add in slippage time for potential delays?

- Project request approved by administration
- Prepare a formal Request for Proposals document that outlines the hardware and RFID tag needs (Reminder: Can you do this independently or will you need to consult with other stakeholders in the library?)
- Go through the bid process to select a vendor
- Put together and charge an implementation team for the conversion project
- Receive hardware/equipment
- Schedule hardware/equipment installation and training
- Hire part-time, short-term staff (or recruit volunteers) to help with retagging the books
- Reduce library hours open to the public and bring all staff on board to help convert the books and catalog records from bar code–based to RFID
- Project completed

4. In the previous exercise, how would you anticipate and plan for the problem of retagging books and converting records that are currently checked out to a library user during the conversion blitz period?

NOTES

1. Bert Spector, *Implementing Organizational Change: Theory and Practice* (New Jersey: Prentice Hall, 2007), 196.
2. Sandra Nelson, *Strategic Planning for Results* (Chicago: American Library Association, 2008), 137.
3. Tupper Cawsey and Gene Deszca, *Toolkit for Organizational Change* (Los Angeles: Sage, 2007), 309.
4. Sandra Nelson, *Implementing for Results* (Chicago: American Library Association, 2009), 161.
5. Joachim C. Brunstein, "Motivation and Performance Following Failure: The Effortful Pursuit of Self-Defining Goals," *Applied Psychology: An International Review* 49, no. 1 (2000): 340–56.
6. Alexandros Paraskevas, "Crisis Management or Crisis Response System: A Complexity Science Approach to Organizational Crisis," *Management Decision* 44, no. 7 (2006): 892–907.
7. G. Hall and S. Hord, "Stages of Concern Questionnaire," in *Implementing Change: Patterns, Principles, and Potholes* (Boston: Allyn and Bacon, 2006), 5.

8. Peter Ruff and Khalid Aziz, *Managing Communications in a Crisis* (Burlington, VT: Gower, 2003).

9. Anthony M. Grant, "Workplace and Executive Coaching: A Bibliography from the Scholarly Business Literature," in *Evidence-Based Coaching Handbook: Putting Best Practices to Work for Your Clients*, ed. Dianne R. Stober and Anthony M. Grant (Hoboken, NJ: Wiley, 2006), 367–89.

10. Dianne R. Stober and Anthony M. Grant, eds., *Evidence-Based Coaching Handbook: Putting Best Practices to Work for Your Clients* (Hoboken, NJ: Wiley, 2006).

11. Christopher Laszlo and Jean-François Laugel, *Large-Scale Organizational Change: An Executive's Guide* (Woburn, MA: Butterworth-Heinemann, 2000), 91.

12. Ruff and Aziz, *Managing Communications in a Crisis*, 87.

13. Robert A. Paton and James McCalman, *Change Management: A Guide to Effective Implementation*, 3rd ed. (London: Sage, 2008), 51.

14. Charles Perrow, *Normal Accidents: Living with High-Risk Technologies* (Princeton, NJ: Princeton University Press, 1999); Matthew Wayne Seeger and others, *Communication and Organizational Crisis* (Westport, CT: Greenwood, 2003).

15. Gerald Lewis, *Organizational Crisis Management: The Human Factor* (New York: Auerbach, 2006), 58.

16. Ruff and Aziz, *Managing Communications in a Crisis*, 35.

17. Susan Carol Curzon, *Managing Change: A How-to-Do-It Manual for Librarians*, rev. ed. (London: Facet, 2006).

18. Kevin M. Morrell and others, "Organizational Change and Employee Turnover," *Personnel Review* 33, no. 2 (2004): 161–73.

19. Ibid.

20. Nelson, *Implementing for Results.*

21. Curzon, *Managing Change.*

22. Alannah E. Rafferty and Mark A. Griffin, "Perceptions of Organizational Change: A Stress and Coping Perspective," *Journal of Applied Psychology* 91, no. 5 (2006): 1154–62; Shaul Oreg, "Personality, Context, and Resistance to Organizational Change," *European Journal of Work and Organizational Psychology* 15, no. 1 (2006): 73–101.

23. Hall and Hord, "Stages of Concern Questionnaire."

24. Mayo Clinic staff, "Seasonal Affective Disorder (SAD)," 2009, www.mayoclinic.com/health/seasonal-affective-disorder/ds00195.

CHAPTER 7 ——————————————————————————————————

MANAGERIAL BAGGAGE

You never get a second chance to make a first impression.

—Will Rogers

IN ADDITION TO organizational culture factors, an individual's effectiveness as a change leader can be affected by the personal experiences and historical baggage that person brings to the table. Montgomery and Cook believe everyday employees, including leaders, bring to work a multitude of abilities and know-how, personal and work-related agendas, physical characteristics and inadequacies, all of which outline a blueprint of their work performance and aspirations.[1] This managerial baggage blueprint was drawn unconsciously over a lifetime of influences and is brought to work every day. It can be seen in how leaders react to different situations, such as organizational change, conflict resolution, and criticism from staff and upper administration. DesRoches indicates that organizations in many ways are a reflection of family systems. He states, "We acknowledge the existence of emotional systems in families, but often ignore emotional realities in the workplace. We act as if people don't have feelings and emotional interactions once they walk through the doors at work, as if these feelings and interactions don't affect the way they do their jobs."[2] As a result, no leader assumes control in a vacuum or with an entirely clean slate. If one has been working within the organization then one has a reputation, deserved or not, for how one will react to a particular set of circumstances. This reputation will vary depending on whether one has been in a department for a long time or has recently transferred in from another area or even another library. Miller believes that long-tenured leaders progressively become more reluctant and even resistant to organizational change because their evolutionary institutionalization has caused them to develop preconceived notions about the organization and they begin to carry more and more "baggage."[3]

Under the umbrella of "succession research," material has been written about leaders who are considered "insiders," those people who were already working for the company and then they became a new leader; and "outsiders," who are considered to be people who were recruited from outside of the company to become a new leader. According to Nodfor and others, the primary difference between an "insider" and an "outsider" is the idea that leaders who come from within the organization are more likely, but not necessarily guaranteed, to think like the outgoing leader because they have been influenced by similar shared experiences.[4] The newly appointed "outsider" leader, on the other hand, would not have these similar shared experiences and would therefore not think like the outgoing leader. However, regardless of whether the successor is from outside or inside the organization, others may try to provide an "introduction" that establishes some initial expectations of how one will lead a change. One aspect of library staff and the librarianship profession is that we are effective at information sharing and networking. However, when one is attempting to lead a change, this networking can complicate the situation and require leaders to successfully adapt their approach to meet the organization's needs.

OUTSIDER WHO IS NEW TO THE LIBRARY

A change manager or leader who is new to the organization will have a very different set of leadership challenges than someone who has been with the organization for a longer period of time. These newer managers represent an unknown to the staff members affected by the change. The staff members are not familiar with the leaders' styles when responding to change-resistant behaviors and whether they tend toward delegating decision making or micromanagement. On the other side of the coin, the change manager does not know how individual staff will respond to change initiatives, which individuals could be grassroots leaders, company protocols, and existing company programs.[5] As explained later in this chapter, this lack of knowledge about each other can be either a positive or a negative in initiating and implementing the change, but must be incorporated into the communication and planning models. Nodfor and others believe that unlike long-tenured leaders, new leaders are more likely to embrace change because they have not been institutionalized by the organizational culture.[6]

Even as there will not be a lot of knowledge about each other, there may be a predisposition to develop assumptions and expectations based on hearsay or limited exposure. Research tells us that people adopt first impressions at first sight.[7] Despite how little time it takes to make this first impression and the limited interaction and data that it is based on, this impression remains virtually unchanged the longer people know one another.[8] As a result, the perception of an individual directs us immediately to a moral judgment without any conscious manifestation or analysis.[9] For example, few new managers or leaders come into an organization without having gone through an interview process. For academic libraries this can be a lengthy process lasting one to two days and covering a wide range of contact between different groups. Based on this interview, both the candidate and the interviewers will form certain opinions of the other. While candidates may not remember specific names and faces, they will take away a general impression of the types of questions that were asked and concerns that seemed to be near the surface. Similarly, after the interview, library employees will share their impressions of the candidate and dissect the interviewee's comments and answers to their questions. However, psychological research suggests that everyone has cognitive biases. These biases cause people to misinterpret new information about a person as a way of sustaining their previous developed impressions of that person.[10] For example, if people believe a leader is not forthright, when that leader communicates to a group that the library needs to change or it will not meet the needs of its users, those with the bias will interpret the information in a way that supports their belief that the leader is not forthright, thus making it more difficult to support the change.

This is why it is critical for a new outside leader during their first meeting to "introduce" one's style and approach in the context of being a leader. For example, suppose Lee is a recently hired unit head and has been directed to improve budget management and tracking licensing processes in the electronic acquisitions operational area. She should use her first several meetings with staff to outline her change leadership style before actually embarking on the specific change initiatives. This would include being up front about the fact that she will be proposing changes, when and in what context she will want feedback and suggestions, how she will go about the decision-making process in formulating her recommendations, and any idiosyncrasies she has in developing relationships. An example of this latter issue might be that, in trying to be open and enthusiastic about ideas, she gives the impression that she is 100 percent behind a suggestion but will then be more evaluative of the idea at a later time. Another example would be letting staff know that she tends to be initially dubious about radical new ideas but will go away and ponder them and come back extremely enthusiastic or wanting to discuss the idea in more detail. Recognizing this about herself and sharing it with her staff will go a long way to establishing a cognitive bias in her staff that she supports an environment with open communication and trust. The staff will know what type of response to expect and will not be left guessing whether she is actually for or against a suggestion; they will not be surprised by an about-face in enthusiasm for an idea, and or wonder whether they are meeting her expectations of them.

During this honeymoon period of getting accustomed to each other, it will be important for leaders to exert a lot of self-discipline to not overreact or precipitate a personalized, emotional response from those around them. Inevitably some staff members will test one's commitment to a leadership style or a set of core values, particularly if they have concerns with the changes one is representing or because the leadership style goes against the employee's cognitive bias. In these cases, grounding oneself in professional courtesy is the best way to build a good foundation for the future. Similarly, even with the emerging grassroots leaders, one should avoid excessive familiarity as it can backfire with an expectation that these staff leaders will have more influence on the final outcome. It also helps one avoid future allegations of letting favoritism influence operational decision making, which in a non-family system would be frowned upon. Because of individual cognitive biases, Montgomery and Cook discuss the importance of managing your relationships at work.[11] They believe that it is critical for leaders (new or old, insider or outsider) to learn how to communicate effectively with everyone, regardless of what cognitive bias they hold. As a result, it may also be good to find a balance that refers to one's previous experience in a way that gives staff members confidence that one knows what one is doing without appearing to overlay the previous experience onto the new organization. Outsiders who consistently refer back to their previous institution as the perfect model of how things should be done at their new institution are examples of failing to communicate effectively in leading change. Instead, one should approach it in an investigative sense of asking whether the experience from the previous institution would be relevant to the new setting.

Because cognitive biases are developed through past life experiences, Porac and others believe that change leaders who come from common backgrounds or the same "cognitive community" have a tendency to possess a set of mutual cognitive biases. These common cognitive community leaders will view their work environments, competition, and leadership roles in like ways and will guide their strategic choices in similar ways.[12] As a result, if the new leader comes from a different cognitive community than the outgoing leader, it is believed that this new leader will implement greater change than a leader of the same cognitive community as the outgoing leader.[13] New leaders need to keep this distinction in mind because many individuals like to feel that they and their institution have some unique positive characteristics or idiosyncrasies. Repeatedly comparing one's current staff model in a negative light to that at another institution as a justification for a change initiative will undermine one's ability to address the organization-specific situational needs in leading the change.

Employees know that simply initiating change for the sake of change will not increase a library's performance. As stated in previous chapters, if employees don't understand why they need to change then they will resist it. According to Nodfor and others, a new leader must conduct a diagnosis or assessment of the organization and determine the changes that are appropriate for a specific situation.[14] Then the new leader must effectively implement these changes. To do this, Hayes studies the use of models in organizational diagnostics. He presents an exercise for change leaders that is intended to facilitate increased awareness of the different diagnosis models leaders employ when examining their organization and evaluating whether or not an organization needs to change.[15] Some of the models discussed by Hayes are popular and more familiar to managers, such as a PEST or SWOT analysis.[16] Other models have less mainstream exposure and may be appropriate to specialized situational assessment, such as Strebel's evolutionary cycle of competitive behavior, Pascale and Athos' 7S Model, Weisbord's six-box organizational model, Kotter's integrative model of organizational dynamics, Nadler and Tushman's congruence model, and the Burke-Litwin causal model of organizational performance and change. Hayes stresses that there are three characteristics that a leader must consider when choosing a diagnostic model.[17] The first is that the model used must be pertinent to the specific issues the leader believes is a problem. The second characteristic is that of picking a model which will help identify cause-and-effect associations for employees. The third characteristic is choosing a model that will help the leader focus on factors that the change leader can affect, rather than measuring factors that are beyond one's ability to currently address.

Another aspect of building one's identity as a change leader is to consider advice from peer managers very carefully. There has already been some discussion about the bias that one can bring to the table as a change leader when one has prior experience in a department or library. As a newcomer, peer managers will often offer one advice about individuals or organizational culture. In some ways this advice can assist one in avoiding land mines that set off a chain reaction or explosion and make the change leadership job all the more difficult. If one knows that particular employees have a tendency to file a grievance whenever they are told to do something that they do not agree with, then the manager can make sure to have lined up one's business operational reasons and documentation when pushing these individuals out of their comfort zones. However, it is also important to recognize that the well-meaning advice can also inhibit an employee's opportunity for a fresh start with a new attitude or perspective.

It may also be that the previous difficulty was as much a function of the advising manager as it was the employee or administrator. Some individuals just rub each other the wrong way because they come from different cognitive communities and find it a constant struggle to communicate effectively. Because of these caveats advice should be welcomed, but received through a personal filter that makes one aware of the potential difficulty and skeptical that the circumstances and personalities guarantee history repeating itself. Thank the advisors politely but remain noncommittal as they tell you how you should handle a particular individual or situation. It is possible for a historically problematic employee to turn around to being a top producer under different leadership that can better understand the motivation and emotions driving this employee. Similarly, where one middle manager may have a strained relationship with an administrator, another may find a positive rapport.

In addition to the challenge of building new relationships with staff and administrators, new change leaders who come from outside the organization will face an additional challenge when it comes to planning the details and troubleshooting the implementation disruptions described in chapter 6. This is because one does not have the organizational knowledge of who are the "go-to" people for resolution. According to Millar and Shamsie, it is imperative for new organizational change leaders to learn as much as they can about their new organization.[18] This learning process will help them develop and increase their human capital within the organization and in so doing enhance their ability to manage organizational change productively. According to Downey, this will not happen overnight, and it could take as long as two to three years for new leaders to truly understand the library and have influence with their staff and to actually accomplish what they were hired to do.[19] This does not mean one cannot implement changes; just that they may need to be on a smaller scale that explicitly addresses a focused issue rather than implementing a large-scale cultural-level change. Additionally, one may not have built up any equity and credibility with supporting players outside the unit operational area, such as human resources or facilities support. In addressing this challenge, building ally relationships with peer managers and members of the administrative support staff will provide one with the connections needed to lead the change. However, because one needs to work through a third party, it is important to realize that it will take longer to resolve issues and collect information than it would for a change leader with a prior background in the organization who knows whom to contact in a crisis.

Having discussed the particular challenges one will face as a newcomer in leading change, it is important to point out that there are advantages to this position as well. One will not have the history or predisposed judgments and assumptions of organizational old-timers and may actually have a better chance of leading a successful change. This is discussed in more detail later in the chapter in the context of the challenges one faces by having an organizational history or reputation. The key factor for a new change leader or manager to recognize is that it may take longer for the change to be implemented because one is in the position of having to learn the organization and build relationships at the same time.

INSIDER WITH HISTORY IN THE LIBRARY

As stated earlier, the foundation of succession research rests on the idea that people from the same library are likely to have similar viewpoints or baggage because of their shared experiences within the library. As a result, it is believed that these shared experiences cause inside successors to think like the outgoing leader. However, since everyone has different experiences and beliefs, leaders do not all come from the same cognitive community. As a result the insider successor may not think like the outgoing leader, going deliberately contrary to the staff's expectations. This would be most likely to occur when the incoming leader feels that an outsider viewpoint was desired by the hiring institutional administrators. Shen and Cannella's empirical study shows, for example, that insiders who assume leadership after effectively challenging and ousting the current leader are more likely to initiate change than another inside successor.[20] This could be why approximately 80 percent of CEO successors in large firms in the United States are insiders.[21] However, Elsaid and Davison argue that if an administration wants to instigate change because the company's performance has been poor, an administration often hires outsiders.[22] Another factor may be one's personal motivation in assuming a leadership position and whether one has a personal need or desire to stand out from one's predecessor. In this situation, initiating change provides one with discrete acts that one can point to as one's own.

In looking at the baggage that one can bring as someone with history in the organization, there are several different parameters that one must take into consideration. How these parameters come together for any one individual may be unique because there is not a single career path model that leads one to become a change leader or manager. But how they interplay can provide insights into approaches for leading successful change initiatives and heading off conflicts. The first factor that must be considered is whether one has experience with the departments primarily impacted by the change, how current that experience is, and the breadth or depth of the experience. A second factor that can be difficult to tease apart from the operational experience is the nature of one's personal relationships with others in the organization, particularly those that will play a significant role in the change initiative or their allies. These are discussed together because if one has actually been in the department for an extended period of time with mature relationships and extensive operational experience, it may not be possible to separate the responsibilities and the roles. The third factor is what experience one has already had in leadership, managerial, or even administrative roles within the organization. However, this last factor is controversial since no one has "connected the philosophy of library services with efficient library management."[23] As a result, traditional MLS programs have tended to focus curriculums on developing their graduates' skills in the traditional functions a librarian would perform, thereby having their graduates learn their management skills on the job. It was only recently that managerial classes were added to some MLS programs.[24] These will all play a role in defining the relationships that one has both with front-line staff and administrators and change the situational and emotional model that one must consider as a leader of a change initiative.

DEPARTMENTAL EXPERIENCE IMPACT

Having department operational experience in the impacted area can be a positive or a negative for a change leader. On the positive side, it reduces one's learning curve in knowledge of the operational area, so one is not constantly having to ask "why" or struggle to understand the area's specific operational jargon.[25] Also, one may already have a sense of who will be enthusiastic about a change and who will need to be won over or ultimately require a more determined or directive approach. One will also have a better sense of each person's style of emotional response, personal motivation, and workplace investment. This would allow the change leader to more readily modify one's communication style to meet an individual staff member's needs. In theory, all of these can make for a smoother transition to getting buy-in and going through the implementation process.

However, there can be drawbacks to having department operational experience as well. Having been immersed in a functional area, particularly if it has been for an extended period of time, may make one less likely to question assumptions about how the area functions and if the unit is doing the "right thing." Proposed ideas may seem radical or incomprehensible because they would push you as well as the operational staff outside of your comfort zones. One warning sign that this has happened is if one is automatically dismissive of or defensive toward a suggestion from someone outside the unit. One can tell oneself that it is because the individual making the suggestion "just does not understand the workflow/processes/rules, and so on," but the truth is that one has gotten too close to the operation to be able to easily lead a major change initiative without an outside catalyst. Another concern comes about because one has formed relationships with the staff in the area. In this situation, one may be less likely to push individuals outside of their comfort zone with new or ongoing, lengthy change initiatives simply because they care too much. Similarly, because one has a sense of where the strongest areas of resistance to the change will occur and who will be involved, one may subconsciously try to work around the individuals or workflows to avoid conflict.[26] This is problematic because it essentially biases one against the individuals with the history of being "difficult" and denies the employees with the resistant history the opportunity to grow and reengage more effectively. It is also a mistake because no matter how much experience one has with a group of employees, every change initiative is different and individual employees can still surprise one with their response to different situational models. Sometimes, those you expect to be on board may have the most difficulty understanding and buying into the change. Alternately, a change you expected to be disturbing to numerous individuals turns out to be a nonissue after all.

Another factor that one has to address is that even as one has impressions of employees based on past performance and responses to previous change initiatives, the same employees will have impressions and knowledge of you that can make it more difficult to lead change. It is an unfortunate aspect of the librarian profession that it is sometimes difficult for individuals in it to let past issues go by the wayside. Some could speculate that this comes from the higher ratio of women to men and their different styles of communicating. According to Tannen's research, author of *You Just Don't Understand: Women and Men in Conversation,* the difference in how women and men communicate goes beyond mere socialization and seems to be intrinsic in the fundamental construct of each sex.[27] It could also come from the nature of the profession and its roots in capturing history and holding knowledge for the future. Whatever the source, there often seems to be a tendency to remember into perpetuity decisions and mistakes one made in the past and refuse to acknowledge that leaders grow, develop, and improve their skills over time. Unfortunately, this can impact one's ability to lead a change initiative as successfully as one would like. If mistakes in the past have undermined the stakeholders' trust in you as a listener or one who empowers staff, then it will be necessary to put extra effort into being sincere about wanting input and transparent about what one is doing with suggestions. Depending on how bad one's mistakes were, restoring trust and confidence may require a significant amount of time and effort on one's part. Similarly, if you have a history of not doing very well in handling disruptions to the plan, this will be an area where you will need to work on controlling your own response and continuing to grow as a change leader. Ferris, Wei, and Zhang believe that insider successors tend to be more optimistic than outsider successors about the future of the firm's performance.[28]

Another unfortunate aspect of staff members knowing you well is that those who are actively against the change can use the information in a manipulative way to sidetrack or derail the change initiative. Suppose Kelly and Rick have been in a department together for ten years. Recently Kelly has been given the change leadership responsibility of introducing more efficiency and accountability into a process Rick is a key stakeholder on, a change Rick is unhappy about and has personalized as questioning his work ethic. Rick knows that in the past, Kelly would get frustrated about administrative interference that appeared to lack an understanding of the workflow and process. To sidetrack Kelly from moving forward on the initiative, Rick uses this knowledge to suggest back that Kelly is doing exactly the same thing, thereby attacking Kelly's value system and confidence as a leader. In this case, Kelly must focus on depersonalizing the change from Rick, explaining the reasons why the change is needed, and giving the change process enough time to really explore the workflow before making any decisions. In the end, Kelly and Rick's relationship may or may not be impacted by their different roles in the change initiative. But it may be something that they do have to address outside of the change itself, thereby introducing an entirely different set of emotions and reactions for them to deal with.

If one has experience in the organization but is a newcomer to the operational area where one is leading the change, one may have a slightly different set of challenges. On the one hand, one has to learn the details of the operational area the same way as a newcomer would. This includes current practices and employee roles. Depending on the organization, one may or may not know the individual staff members in the department. If the organization is one that has encouraged cross-departmental teams and social and professional interactions across the staff as a whole, then experienced individuals will have some knowledge of those they will be leading. Alternately, one may know some of them at a superficial level but not the others. This is particularly tricky because it is a natural tendency to approach those we are comfortable with first when engaging or testing out an idea. However, this will quickly open the door to perceptual favoritism if these individuals are not recognized by others as the grassroots or hierarchical leaders within the department.

Additionally, one will be facing a variation of the familiarity issue discussed previously, where one may have preconceived opinions of employees or they may have preconceived opinions of you based on hearsay and the organizational grapevine. In some ways, depending on what everyone has heard about each other creates a situation that is even more difficult than either of the other models previously discussed. Unlike the newcomer, one does have a history but unlike the experienced individual, one may not understand one's reputation because it is not a response to firsthand knowledge. In this case, one may want to used a blended approach of addressing the rumors about you directly, possibly even asking what people have heard or what opinions they already have, and follow up with the type of "self-introduction" that was mentioned for the organizational newcomer. One thing to be careful of in this situation is to not appear to be criticizing one's previous peers or their perception of you. It is better to fall back on generalities such as "I know that some people find my leadership style a difficult one," "I have had philosophical conflicts with some individuals in the past," or simply admit to not having addressed a particular situation as well in the past as you would try to do now, given time, experience, and your own personal growth.

LEADERSHIP EXPERIENCE IMPACT

One final factor in taking on a change leader or change manager role when one has history in the organization is whether one's history is as a peer or leader or both and the time in rank as a manager or leader. If you are leading a change initiative among individuals who were recently at a peer level, you will have to step a bit more carefully in maintaining a positive relationship once the change initiative is completed. This is particularly critical when one is only temporarily a change leader, such as for an ad hoc team, and does not have a formalized, hierarchical managerial role accompanying the change leadership responsibilities. In this case, one will have to strongly focus on reaching consensus in commitment to the idea of the change before actually implementing it. Otherwise, one can create an environment that will actually be hostile to go back to in having overridden one's peers. Because one does not have the authority to ultimately direct others to cooperate with the idea, it is best to start out with smaller scale, less controversial changes for the temporary or ad hoc leadership model. Unfortunately, this may not always be possible if one has a secondary skill set that positions one to be the obvious leader of a major new initiative, even if it is controversial. This is often the case with new service initiatives, particularly when they involve technology where one may have more immersive knowledge than the "official" managers. Thinking about the earlier example with Rick and Kelly, Rick might be less likely to play the emotional manipulation card if Kelly has actually been promoted into a department head or titled leadership role, which often forces changes in interpersonal dynamics.

If one is new to a leadership role or attempting to lead a larger or more controversial initiative as a temporary leader, it may be a good technique to include either a manager from another area or a senior grassroots leader at your side on any key planning or implementation teams. This person can back you up in representing and interpreting the administrative perspective in the event someone challenges your authority or tries to position you as a target for his or her frustrations with the proposed change. This is particularly a consideration if one is part of a formal tenure and promotion system where employees impacted by the change will be in a position to directly influence a future promotion opportunity. While one would hope that professionals would rise above holding an untenured faculty member responsible for what is actually an administrative initiative, when emotions are engaged the issues become much more complex. There are several important characteristics to consider in choosing an individual to protect your back and provide you with constructive feedback on developing as a leader. First, does the individual have the same general approach to change leadership as you do? This does not mean you have to agree on every aspect of leadership, but the supporting individual needs to agree on the value of seeking input and communicating with affected employees. If the experienced individual is more embedded in a traditional, hierarchical approach to directing change from a position of absolute authority, this person will not do well in supporting you as an empowering change leader. Second, do the employees impacted by the change respect the backup leader or manager? This is important because in order to be supportive of you, the individual needs to have personal equity or a solid, positive reputation built up with the impacted stakeholders. If the stakeholders do not respect the individual, your job as a change leader will be all the more difficult because of a "guilt by association" perspective. Third, are you comfortable with the individual and trust that the individual will step back and let you take a leadership role, but provide you with support and guidance when you need it? This can actually be the most difficult characteristic to determine because one cannot entirely predict the challenges that both of you will encounter in your trying to lead the change. It can be helpful to have a frank and open discussion with the individual in order to clarify expectations before confirming the individual's commitment. This discussion should address style preferences for feedback and intervention. For instance, do you want to set a code phrase for the more senior change leader to use if observing that you are about to do something that could mean a major setback in building buy-in, a phrase that cues you to back off and defer a comment until you can discuss it with the individual later? Or are you comfortable with the individual jumping in with a counterproposal or difference of opinion on the spot? Do you need the individual to give you positive encouragement ahead of informing you about areas for improvement, or are you more comfortable glossing over praise and going directly to constructive comments on how you can improve your communications and decisions as a change leader? These are important issues to decide before one is "on the stage" in front of others, because if either of you becomes uncomfortable with the dynamics or it appears you are in conflict with each other, it will make others uncomfortable as well and undermine their commitment to you as a leader.

While building buy-in is always important, a change leader who is also in a managerial role is able to take more hierarchical responsibility for implementing the change. Authoritative leadership does not mean one should use one's managerial authority to override concerns but does allow one to be more definite about administrative support for the change. The managerial title also creates a bit of space between the leader and the stakeholders and can help minimize personal conflicts. Within much of our society, programmed from our grade school days, one respects the teacher or manager role with an assumption that the person has done something to be put in charge. This does not mean that one cannot lose the respect of one's employees, but the initial assumption is that one is a competent leader, which can help others keep an open mind as you ask them to step outside their comfort zone. Last but not least, a formal manager as the change leader can apply the organization's performance evaluation and disciplinary models if necessary as a motivational factor toward an employee's engagement on change initiatives.

If one has been in a managerial position for some time, one does need to take care that one's formal title and past performance on other managerial activities is not inhibiting feedback and input about the change. This is where history can have a major impact on one's ability to effect an empowered and emotionally engaged workforce. Because one is in the position of reflecting how an employee did in a performance evaluation, one has to go the extra mile in creating a "safe" environment where employees feel they can speak up with their concerns without either being labeled uncooperative or appearing incompetent to their supervisor. This is particularly difficult when one is asking individuals to move outside of their comfort zone into a situation where emotions are near the surface and value systems more exposed. One may feel that one has an open door policy, but has one's communication style created an environment where staff members feel comfortable taking advantage of it? Or do you send out the invitation and either no one or only the same repeaters come? This latter is a clear warning that one will likely encounter difficulty trying to lead change with empowerment and emotional engagement because one really does not know how those impacted by the change are thinking or feeling.

If one is a new manager, one faces additional scrutiny that can undermine one's confidence as a change leader or lead to rushed, bad decision making. Depending on the circumstances that led you to be appointed to the managerial ranks, you may feel that administrators are watching and testing you more than they would be for a more experienced manager. In this case, it will be important to stay connected to get regular feedback from a mentor or one's immediate reporting administrator. In truth, most administrators will be expecting you to make some mistakes that are typical of a new manager and are more interested in how you correct the mistakes or make situational adjustments. Depending on personal coaching style, the administrator may caution you not to be too hasty or pushy in how you approach a situation or individual or may encourage you to keep moving right along with the change, knowing it will be a growth experience. This is not intended to question a new manager's competence, but to suggest experience has shown that effectively leading a successful change initiative is usually a slower process than one would like it to be.

Depending on departmental history and prior interactions, new managers may also feel that staff are watching or testing them. In a sense this may be true, and it will be important to think seriously about one's leadership values and how one wants to establish one's leadership style early on. This includes establishing the professional persona that one shows the world and developing professional knowledge of individuals; the latter allows one to avoid seeing an individual as an anonymous resource or entry in a spreadsheet or block on a workflow, and it also allows one to avoid getting drawn into an employee's personal lifestyle challenges and drama. Then one can use some of the same techniques described earlier in the chapter for someone new to the institution, but with the focus of being new to management and still developing as a leader. Downey believes that all new leaders (insiders and outsiders) grapple with the problem of how much they should draw on their past leadership experience and how much they should be amenable to learning new paradigms.[29] It is important for new leaders to remember that if they rely too much on their past experiences, they will hamper their integration into the new leadership role. This is because they are assessing situations and acting on these situations based on past beliefs and assumptions that may no longer be true. The main thing to keep in mind if one is new to leading change is that one will make mistakes through the process. Knowing this, one should plan ahead how to recognize when one has misstepped and have a recovery plan to move forward from it.

In interacting with staff, an experienced manager faces a different challenge, one based on having a clearly established professional identity and reputation. Because they are mature managers who have faced and grown from leadership challenges in the past, experienced managers may be much more set in their management styles. For them, changing their communication or leadership style to create an environment that supports positive change can be difficult. Part of the difficulty comes in rec-ognizing how others see one and consciously considering how this impacts one's effectiveness as a change leader, not necessarily an easy task. Some techniques to follow in gaining this knowledge are similar to the techniques of communicating on the change initiative, though in this case the "change" is to the manager's leadership style. One should ask peers and grassroots leaders what their impression is of your leadership. If individuals are not able to share their perspectives of your leadership, such as on decision making, in a clearly communicated and transparent manner, this is an indication that you have already put the success of the project at risk by inhibit-ing engagement and may need to do some self-analysis and address some issues from a new leadership perspective before embarking on the actual change project. This will be particularly awkward if you have done something in the recent past that has actually damaged the trust relationship your employees have with you. In this case, you will need to convince employees that you have changed, recognizing that actions speak louder than words.

Whatever the operational or leadership history that one has, the key is to be aware of the potential advantages or drawbacks and factor them into communication and planning for the change initiative.[30] If one has a really strong reputation established as a positive and successful change leader who engages effectively with impacted employees, one will not need to work as hard at building buy-in and confidence in the proposed change as either a new change leader or a change leader that has a damaged trust relationship. If one is new, then one needs to factor in time to learn enough of the operation to be able to have substantive discussions on stakeholder concerns and establish a relationship of trust that encourages empowerment. If one has a strained or damaged trust relationship, then one is going to have to go to extra lengths to build confidence in the proposed change. Otherwise, the initiative has a higher probability of not meeting expectations for success or even falling into the failure category. Ulti-mately, as one begins a new change initiative, one needs to focus on being agile and responsive to the situational leadership needs created by the response of the stakehold-ers to the explanation and implementation of the project.

CAUGHT IN THE MIDDLE

Regardless of whether one has experience or is new to leadership or whether one is an insider or outsider, it is important as a change leader to make sure you do not get caught in the middle, even if one is a middle manager. This can occur if one has administrative leadership in the organization who are highly directive but have poor communication or conflict management skills and have high aspirations for organizational change taking place within a short time window. It can also occur if the administrative leadership prescribes a strongly hierarchical management model that does not allow for the empowerment and emotional engagement discussed in this book. In this case, it is important to be extremely careful when one is following administrative dictates and walk a tightrope that balances one between supporting staff as they are asked to follow irrational-appearing dictates and cajoling them to go along with the administration's initiatives. With administrators one will have to recognize where one can influence the timing or progression of a change initiative and when the battle is not worth fighting. The key thing is to make sure to maintain a bit more distance from administration. This does not mean one should be constantly, publicly blaming administrators for having to change things, as that is the quickest path to being perceived as a weak or ineffective manager. Rather, one can use grassroots leaders to spread the word that one is trying to negotiate with administrators and does sympathize with employees' frustrations even as one may find it necessary to publicly support the administrative position. Similarly, you should keep your professional goals in mind, and you may find it necessary to deliberatively choose a different approach as a change leader to avoid becoming an organizational scapegoat for an unpopular change.

KEYS TO SUCCESS

In recognizing the importance of your history and the preconceived assumptions others have of your leadership and communication style, there are several techniques one can apply in addressing one's managerial baggage.

- Be honest with yourself about your leadership strengths, weaknesses, and idiosyncrasies and consider how they will impact your ability to lead the change initiative.
- Work to identify any assumptions others have about you as a leader that could inhibit empowerment and engagement on the change initiative.
- Address directly misconceptions, historical misunderstandings, or unsuccessful changes by placing them in the context of time, growth, or environment.
- Be willing to adapt your leadership style to the situational needs of the stakeholders and change process.
- Do not be afraid to admit to being human and making mistakes.

THINKING EXERCISES

1. Reflect on what your history has been at your current organization. What managerial baggage do you have with your staff? What about with administrators above you or peer managers?

2. If you were to announce that you would be leading a new change initiative tomorrow, do you know how the message would be received at an emotional level? Would stakeholders expect to have a participatory role in making the change happen?

3. If your previous change leadership style ran counter to the models and techniques described in this book, how will you go about engaging with others in a way that does not get caught up in your leadership history?

4. What particular challenges do you think you would encounter in "reinventing" yourself without going to a new organization?

5. If you were (or are) new to the organization, what techniques will you use to dispel assumptions others may have already leaped to about your leadership style? If you did not feel you have a reputation to overcome, how would you begin and set a future course for leading change?

NOTES

1. Jack G. Montgomery and Eleanor I. Cook, *Conflict Management for Libraries: Strategies for a Positive, Productive Workplace* (Chicago: American Library Association, 2005).
2. Brian DesRoches, *Your Boss Is Not Your Mother: Breaking Free from Emotional Politics to Achieve Independence and Success at Work* (New York: Morrow, 1995), xii.
3. Danny Miller, "Stale in the Saddle: CEO Tenure and the Match between Organization and Environment," *Management Science* 37, no. 1 (1991): 34–52.
4. Hermann Achidi Nodfor and others, "What Does the New Boss Think? How New Leaders' Cognitive Communities and Recent 'Top Down' Success Affect Organizational Change and Performance," *Leadership Quarterly* 20 (2009): 799–813.
5. Diane Downey, "HR's Role in Assimilating New Leaders," *Employment Relations Today*, Winter 2002, 69–83.
6. Nodfor, "What Does the New Boss Think?"
7. L. Albright, D. A. Kenny, and T. E. Malloy, "Consensus in Personality Judgments at Zero Acquaintance," *Journal of Personality and Social Psychology* 55 (1988): 387–95.
8. N. Ambady and R. Rosenthal, "Thin Slices of Expressive Behavior as Predictors of Interpersonal Consequences: A Meta-Analysis," *Psychological Bulletin* 11 (1992): 256–74.
9. Jonathan Haidt, "The Emotional Dog and Its Rational Tail: A Social Intuitionist Approach to Moral Judgment," *Psychological Review* 108, no. 4 (2001): 814–34.

10. Matthew Rabin and Joel L. Schrag, "First Impressions Matter: A Model of Confirmatory Bias," *Quarterly Journal of Economics* 114, no. 1 (1999): 37–82.
11. Montgomery and Cook, *Conflict Management for Libraries.*
12. Joseph F. Porac, Howard Thomas, and Charles Baden-Fuller, "Competitive Groups as Cognitive Communities: The Case of Scottish Knitwear Manufacturers," *Journal of Management Studies* 26, no. 4 (2007): 397–416.
13. Nodfor, "What Does the New Boss Think?" 799–813.
14. Ibid.
15. John Hayes, *The Theory and Practice of Change Management*, 3rd ed. (Basingstoke, NY: Palgrave Macmillan, 2010).
16. Ibid.
17. Ibid.
18. Danny Miller and Jamal Shamsie, "Learning across the Life Cycle: Experimentation and Performance among Hollywood Studio Heads," *Strategic Management Journal* 22, no. 8 (2001): 725–45.
19. Downey, "HR's Role in Assimilating New Leaders."
20. Wei Shen and Albert A. Cannella Jr., "Revisiting the Performance Consequences of CEO Succession: The Impacts of Succession Type, Post-Succession Senior Executive Turnover, and Departing CEO Tenure," *Academy of Management Journal* 45, no. 4 (2002): 717–33.
21. Anup Agrawal, Charles R. Knoeber, and Theofanis Tsoulouhas, "Are Outsiders Handicapped in CEO Successions?" *Journal of Corporate Finance* 12 (2006): 619–44.
22. Eahab Elsaid and Wallace N. Davison, "What Happened to CEO Compensation Following Turnover and Succession?" *Quarterly Review of Economics and Finance* 49, no. 2 (2009): 424–47.
23. Wayne A. Wiegand and Donald G. Davis, *Encyclopedia of Library History* (New York: Garland, 1994), 374.
24. Montgomery and Cook, *Conflict Management for Libraries*, 180.
25. Downey, "HR's Role in Assimilating New Leaders."
26. Alison Rieple, "The Paradoxes of New Managers as Levers of Organizational Change," *Strategic Change* 7 (1997): 211–25.
27. Deborah Tannen, "Women and Men in Conversations," in *The Workings of Language: From Prescriptions to Perspectives*, ed. Rebecca S. Wheeler (Westport, CT: Praeger, 1999), 211–16.
28. Stephen P. Ferris, Zuobao Wei, and Shaorong Zhang. "CEO Succession, Incentives and Firm Performance: Insiders versus Outsiders," http://69.175.2.130/~finman/Orlando/Papers/CEO_FWZ_07.pdf.
29. Downey, "HR's Role in Assimilating New Leaders."
30. Nodfor, "What Does the New Boss Think?"

CHAPTER 8

EVALUATING THE CHANGE AND YOURSELF AS A CHANGE LEADER

Fear cannot be banished, but it can be calm and without panic; it can be mitigated by reason and evaluation.

—Vannevar Bush

IN EVALUATING THE success and effectiveness of yourself in a change leadership role and the results of the change itself, there is a temptation to take the quick and easy, big picture approach. This is accomplished by answering a few basic questions about the change initiative. Was it accomplished more or less on schedule? Do employees appear to have moved past their emotions and reengaged in the work of the library? Were grievances or complaints kept to a minimum? Are others in the organization speaking comfortably with you? Have library users given some positive feedback about the change? If the answers are yes, then one can assume the change was successful, right? Wrong. Assessing the success of the change and evaluating yourself as a leader of change are much more complex than that. One has to look at whether the change truly accomplished what was established as the purpose of it and whether it correlates to the standards of the institution. Another factor to consider is looking at the long-term impact of the organizational investment in the change and how deeply the change becomes integrated into the culture and operations of the organization, as well as what its long-term impact was on the employee workload. One also needs to examine the residual emotional effect on both the leader and impacted employees. If you as a leader are exhausted from having led the change, then you may not have been quite as effective as you thought you were. Similarly, staff recoiling in horror, refusing to meet your gaze or greet you in the hall, or gazing at you in a state of glazed numbness at the announcement of the next change are other indicators that all has not been as successful as you may have thought. This chapter will look at the importance of truly assessing the success of a change initiative and your performance as the leader of it from the business and human resources literature and provide some tips on how to accomplish this.

AVOIDING THE POSTMORTEM

As mentioned earlier in the book, most administrators, not just those in a library setting, tend to neglect to incorporate evaluation measures into their organizational change processes. It is believed that most administrators not only do not know how to evaluate programs or changes, but they do not understand the advantages of what these evaluations can do for them and the institution they work for. Russ-Eft and Preskill state that there are ten primary reasons why the evaluation process is neglected.[1]

- The evaluation was not asked for.
- Bad past experiences with evaluation.
- Leaders believe they already know what does and does not work.
- Management believes that the cost of the evaluation process outweighs the benefits.
- Conducting an evaluation is seen as being too much work.
- Belief that the evaluation results will not be used.
- Evaluation is considered an afterthought.
- Lack of evaluation skills.
- Fear of the impact of the evaluation results.
- Misunderstanding of the evaluation's intention.

Subsequent material provided in this chapter speaks to several of these points, particularly to respond to a lack of knowledge or misunderstanding of what, why, and how change initiatives and change leadership can be evaluated.

On the rare occasions when an evaluation is carried out, it is generally handled like an addendum or afterthought to a project instead of a deliberative planning tool for future improvements. In many libraries, by the time the leadership has reached the evaluation stage of the process, they are already involved in another change initiative and have already mentally and emotionally moved on from the previous, "completed" change. In this mindset, the evaluation process is not seen as something that will yield valuable information that could be used in carrying forward the next change initiative more effectively, but rather as a tool to define closure. The evaluation may consist of a satisfaction survey sent to library users or staff members or an open meeting led by the change leader to "give feedback." On occasion, this latter event may actually be folded into a "celebration" at accomplishing the change with punch and cake, thereby sending a hidden message that critical or negative comments are not actually being sought as they would spoil the mood. This represents a misunderstanding of the true potential of assessment. The purpose of an evaluation may vary, but the reason for conducting the evaluation itself should be to see how something, such as a program, workflow, or process, can be or was improved.[2]

This mirrors much of what is being done regarding assessment in higher education as a whole. Long focused on the end-of-term student evaluations for courses with a few major exams and perhaps a single paper leading to a final grade as the assessment mechanism, there has been a shifting paradigm to recognize that in many ways this level of evaluation is inadequate. By the time the course instructor would receive the evaluation comments or be assigning final grades, the course is over, students have moved on, and the instructor is working on the next term's course, which may be an entirely different topic. Instead there is now more emphasis on assessing student understanding and progress in more ongoing and snapshot ways through the entire term. This is done through more interim assessment techniques that may be formal or informal. Some formal techniques include more frequent exams over less material, or more reflective critical thinking exercises or discussion activities that better gauge actual understanding. Some informal techniques may include brief discussions at the beginning or end of a class or quick shows of hands, "clicker" surveys, or speed writing feedback. Change leaders in libraries can adapt some of these assessment techniques during the course of the change to get a better sense of whether it really is moving along effectively or whether one is simply missing some cues that there are festering issues that could undermine or slow down the eventual success of the change.

WHAT IS EVALUATION?

Although there is a debate among scholars about the actual definition of the term *evaluation*, the perspective of Boulmetis and Dutwin seems appropriate to the context here. These researchers believe there are two very similar but different definitions of evaluation: "[1] Evaluation is the systematic process of collecting and analyzing data in order to determine whether and to what degree objectives have been or are being achieved. [2] Evaluation is the systematic process of collecting and analyzing data in order to make a decision." Although the two definitions are similar, the focus behind each definition is very different and depends on the purpose of the evaluation.[3] Both of these definitions play a role when one is evaluating a change initiative. The first definition is a key part of determining whether the change ultimately accomplished the original intended goal, or whether it got off track. In some cases, the goal itself may have changed during the period of implementation. In this case, one has to evaluate what the accomplishment and ultimate redefined purpose of the change was and what its value was to the institution.

The definition plays into the philosophy that there is always room for improvement, particularly with something that is as challenging as leading a change initiative. It is important in assessing change and leadership to assess areas that have relevance and transferability to future change initiatives. In this way, one may want to focus less on the explicit details of the change that would make it unique from the specific department's perspective and focus more on the process and organizational culture elements that will continue past the basic implementation. When taken together, these definitions build a learning model that allows for the results of the first definition, which is closer to the project closure concept, to be used in decision making of the second definition in leading employees and users through the next change process.

Scriven believes that there are two common purposes that describe evaluation activities: summative and formative.[4] In the first definition of evaluation above, one can determine that the evaluator is collecting the data at the end of the organizational change or the implementation of a new library service. The primary motivation is to validate that the change was successful and what its long-term impact will be on the organization.[5] This is often referred to as a summative evaluation. According to Scriven, this evaluation is best carried out by external evaluators (such as a granting agency or university office outside the library) and usually occurs at the end of the organizational change.[6] In a library setting, a summative evaluation can be equated to a university auditor evaluating a library's acquisition accounting workflow to make sure it is secure. However, few libraries will engage with an outside party for assessment of smaller operations-based changes. In this model, *external* could be identified as someone that was not a primary or secondary stakeholder of the change—in essence a neutral party—to come in and do an assessment on how well the change was accomplished. This individual might conduct focus groups with stakeholders or invite feedback on what was done successfully or what might need to be improved.

According to Russ-Eft and Preskill, there are four general types of summative evaluations: monitoring and auditing, outcome evaluation, impact evaluation, and performance measurement.[7] Monitoring and auditing is a type of summative evaluation that focuses on making sure that the organizational change is implemented the way it was designed and agreed upon by all participating parties.[8] It will be important to be more precise in what information one gathers in assessing the "success" of the initiative. A change that went through a significant amount of redefinition during the planning or implementation process or faced significant unexpected crises may be more difficult to evaluate than a more straightforward change where the planning and implementation were accomplished in a linear and straightforward manner. Outcome evaluation focuses on understanding the proposed outcomes of the organizational change to see what benefits this change has on employees' "knowledge, attitudes, values, skills, behavior, condition, or status."[9] Closely related to outcome evaluation is impact evaluation, which focuses on the effect the organizational change had on the employees. This is generally done by estimating what could happen if the change were not made in comparison to what happened when the change was made. The fourth type of summative evaluation is the performance measurement, which focuses on change activities such as the outcomes of a newly implemented library service. The tendency of most libraries is to focus on the first and fourth type of summative evaluation, verifying that the change happened as it was intended and evaluating the change in terms of the external users or customers. Evaluating the change as it relates to employees is often overlooked or marginalized under the guise of employees just having to do what is "necessary" to implement the change. However, it is this area that can play such a significant part in employees' successful engagement upon the announcement of the next change initiative.

Boulmetis and Dutwin's second definition of evaluation above focuses on the importance of change to the whole of the organization and how the organization can improve. In addition to using summative information from previous changes as a learning tool, it offers the option for the evaluation activities to occur at any stage in the life of an organizational change or service implementation. Consequently, an evaluation might occur when the administration is considering implementing a new reference service and they have the change leader conduct a needs assessment to see if the new service is needed to help improve user satisfaction. The change leader's responsibility during a needs assessment is to ask not only the library employees but also the library patrons questions to see if the change is really needed.[10] There is nothing more frustrating to employees than when administration tells them they need to change a work process without their input. When this top-down edict occurs, employees feel shut out of the process and begin to feel resentful toward the administration and the proposed change because it is the employees who understand their day-to-day workflow and its problems, not the administrators who see from a distance and do not understand the day-to-day running of library. As a result, this creates increasing resentment, which could develop into a hostile organizational environment that is automatically distrusting and resentful of the change. It is important for the change leader to work in conjunction with the employees so that the change leader can get accurate feedback in order to implement a successful organizational change.[11]

Evaluation can also occur during the planning stage of the organizational change where the change leader could develop evaluation activities that would center on the implementation. In addition, during the implementation period of the organizational change, the change leader might establish an evaluation activity to scrutinize change outcomes that would help identify impact measurement that could affect the library's future and it projected accomplishments.[12] This situation is often referred to as a formative evaluation, which Scriven defines as "typically conducted during the development or improvement of a program or product (or person, and so on) and it is conducted, often more than once, for the in-house staff of the program with the intent to improve."[13] Unlike the summative evaluations, which are primarily done by external evaluators, formative evaluations are usually conducted by internal library evaluators. However, what is interesting about the formative evaluation results is that they are injected back into the organizational change so that this new information might develop increased positive results, while refining and ultimately correcting the change process to meet the change program goals.

At this point, a change leader could be expressing dismay at the suggestion that in addition to all of the previously mentioned communication and emotional engagement, one is also charged with carrying out ongoing assessments with the various staff member stakeholders, adding in a lot of evaluation activities to an already heavy workload. This is actually similar to the responses that many teaching faculty have had to adding more outcomes assessment to their courses. However, as mentioned earlier, not all formative evaluations conducted during the process of the change initiative need be extensive formalized models, with intensive data gathering and analysis. They might be as simple as meetings designed and conducted to collect feedback, quick surveys of half a dozen or less straightforward questions to gauge understanding, buy-in, and engagement on a particular part of the change, or a single contemplative, short-answer question to prompt creative suggestions on tackling a particular problem. The key is that one is receptive to the responses in moving activities forward.

Regardless of the purpose of the evaluation, the importance of using the evaluation findings is critical. It is important for leaders to consider ahead of time how they will use the results from the evaluation activity, particularly as these will inevitably reflect some information the leader did not anticipate or want to see, such as a lack of support for a particular element of the change initiative or a suggested approach that is diametrically opposite from what the leader expects. Some would suggest this is erroneously assuming a negative response, particularly if one has been effective as a leader in communicating the purpose of the change and including stakeholders actively in the planning and implementation process. In this case, could not a leader reasonably expect the evaluation results to correspond to or validate what the change leader was already planning to do? While one could expect the results to be more consistent and generally supportive, one should consider the basics of group dynamics. Even as they are engaged in the change process, few stakeholders will be as immersed in understanding the change initiative as thoroughly as the change leader. Similarly, any time a group is brought together there will be ideas that any one individual will not have considered. Finally, even as one thinks one is doing an excellent job at leading the change, even the best and most experienced manager can still be surprised by staff members and their thoughts on an issue. Because of these factors, change leaders must expect that at some point of the process, other employees will have suggestions or ideas that differ from the leader's grand plan for the change. When faced with this, one should step back to the techniques referenced earlier in this book to reopen communications and engagement and reconsider if one is doing the "right" thing.

From a staff member's perspective there is nothing worse than having spent her time and efforts on providing or collecting information for an evaluation activity only to discover that the information is ignored or misinterpreted when it goes counter to the supervisor's expectations. This creates distrust between the employees and administration and could create resistance among the employees toward the organizational change. In library settings, program evaluations are used extensively to scrutinize everything from how a librarian teaches a library instruction class to customer satisfaction on old and new services offered by the library. Many scholars believe that program evaluation is meant "to determine if a program is any good."[14] In truth there are many other nuances to evaluation that enter into play when using different evaluation models or tools. However, it becomes a challenge for a library change leader to decide on which evaluation model should be used to evaluate a new organizational change.

EVALUATION MODELS

Once the decision is made to perform a summative or formative evaluation process, it is important for change leaders or evaluators to decide on an evaluation model they are going to use. Deciding on an evaluation model helps everyone involved in the change think about what they are being asked to do and how to do it efficiently. However, despite the complexity of many evaluation models, change leaders should have some fundamental understanding of the commonly used models so that they can choose which one they should use for their evaluation requirements. According to Boulmetis and Dutwin, there are five commonly used evaluation models: system analysis/decision-making model, transaction model, goal-free model, discrepancy model, and objective attainment model.[15] Each of these is briefly presented below with the context of a possible application in a library change initiative.

STUFFLEBEAM'S SYSTEM ANALYSIS MODEL OR DECISION-MAKING EVALUATION MODEL

The decision-making evaluation model was originally designed by Daniel Stufflebeam in 1971 and focuses the evaluator's attention on the decisions that need to be made in the future about the use of a new service or organizational change. Instead of worrying about how the new service is currently operating, the evaluator uses the decision-making model of evaluation to make decisions about the long-range effects of a new service or program. In libraries today administrators are faced with "what if" scenarios around the format of monographs. Should they focus their acquisition budgets on e-books readable only through their personal computers, or should they look at e-books that are viewable using e-readers? However, change leaders need to make sure they are not chasing a vision before its time. According to Conger, sometimes a leader's view of the future is too optimistic and becomes ahead of its time, and as a result patrons fail to uphold the change leader's plan.[16] The decision-making process involves three steps. First, the evaluator must outline what information needs to be gathered. Second, the evaluator must gather the needed information. Third, the evaluator must provide the information to the decision makers.[17]

STAKE'S TRANSACTION EVALUATION MODEL

Created by R. E. Stake in 1975, the transaction evaluation model focuses on dialogue throughout the evaluation process between the organizational change leader and affected staff members.[18] This model is the one most frequently overlooked or misunderstood as a top-down communication model rather than a dialogue for assessment. To develop this constant feedback, the organizational change leader can use a number of observational and interview methods to gain the needed evaluation information from the staff and patrons. While an individual or even a team cannot anticipate every detail that will come out of a change initiative, missing something that has a significant impact on the effectiveness of the change or the staff and other processes is an indicator that one did not listen and engage effectively in addressing employee concerns or one rushed the change through. This is also true if one discovers that the change is not well supported by the current infrastructure after implementation.[19] An example of this might be implementing a new policy of loading bulk records into the library catalog for purchased electronic collections, only to discover that the bulk load module for one's integrated library system is weakly designed and it will require extensive staff resources to bring the records up to an acceptable level of quality after the load. This would have a significant effect on the departmental workload and differs from overlooking minor details that need to be adjusted as the change initiative is implemented.

However, the transaction evaluation model will work only if leaders listen to their employees and admit to flaws in their strategic vision, and if their employees tell them the truth. According to Conger, leaders may recognize that their vision is producing negative results, but they continue because they don't want to tarnish their perception of themselves by stopping the change initiative. Adding to this problem, employees who are intimidated by their change leader fear that speaking up will bring negative repercussions on them; conversely, there are those who idealize their leader excessively to the point where they themselves do not see the flaws in the change plan. As a result, they continue working on their leader's instructions regardless of their negative feelings or concerns.[20] If the organizational culture has trust issues or employees seem hesitant to speak up, then using anonymous-response, ballot-style boxes to gather information on feedback and concerns can be a useful technique—particularly if one then posts the questions and responses to them so that everyone who might be quietly sharing the same idea can see the response. While this is a less efficient way of communicating than an open dialogue, it can be useful in putting people more at ease and demonstrating a commitment to being open to ideas and suggestions.

This model can also be undermined by staff giving feedback based on fear-driven, worst-case-scenario suppositions. In this case, they may be embellishing their feedback with half-truths or outright inaccuracies. A warning sign that an employee may be less effective in this model is when "but what if" is scattered in their comments. A leader may need to sit down and actually follow up with a dialogue that brings the inaccuracies to light in order to clarify what is and is not being done.

SCRIVEN'S GOAL-FREE EVALUATION MODEL

Developed in the early 1970s by Michael Scriven, the foundation of the goal-free model rests on the actual effects of the organizational change divorced from any preconceived notions of what the original organizational goals were. What this means is that unlike the discrepancy evaluation model mentioned previously, Scriven's model does not base its evaluation on any set standards or goals, nor does the evaluator have any preconceived notions of how the organizational change will affect the library.[21] Instead, in order to create an unbiased decision and thereby prevent tunnel vision, the goal-free evaluation model looks at the actual outcome of the change regardless of its goals to see if the effects of the change on the organization address the overall organizational needs.[22] By doing this, the change manager does not focus only on the anticipated goals and will not jeopardize the full results by failing to notice other positive or negative unplanned side effects of the change.[23] The evaluator needs to gather the data using both obtrusive techniques, such as interviewing patrons and staff, and unobtrusive techniques, such as reviewing usage data or frequency of requests, in order to make fair and unbiased decisions about what was actually accomplished with the organizational change.

The goal-free evaluation model is a good model for those organizations that have a "visionary leader" who will initiate change based on a personal, intuitive approach of what is needed. Sadly, these leaders tend to be so committed to the perspective that feels so right to them that they often fail to listen to their employees. Problems arise when these needs and beliefs are disconnected from the needs and beliefs of the library patrons. These leaders do everything; even disregard the repercussions of losing the respect of staff and library patrons, to achieve their personal vision. Using the goal-free evaluation model makes it more difficult for leaders to fall back on their biases or tunnel vision.[24] The enthusiastic but well-intended intuitive leader will recognize from the evaluation results where the initiatives have not had the expected impact and can learn from the experience to temper the ideas with input from others. Those that persist in their vision in the face of clear evidence to the contrary will be revealed more clearly as the poor leaders they are, leading to their own lowered performance ratings.

PROVUS DISCREPANCY EVALUATION MODEL

Designed by Malcolm Provus in 1969, the foundation of the discrepancy model rests on the idea that change does not live in a vacuum but rather is part of a complex system. Provus believed that in order to evaluate a complex organizational change, the evaluator must first agree upon performance standards on how the change should work. Once these standards are established, any discrepancy discovered between the pre- and postorganizational change periods would identify weaknesses in the change itself. This weakness would determine if improvements were needed or if the change was to continue or be abandoned.[25] This model effectively determines if the change is staying on track to the purpose of its initial inception. As an example, suppose the library decided to enact a change initiative to develop and implement a new service intended to meet the needs of its distance education patrons based on a performance standard focused on great customer service. While conducting an assessment of the requirements to implement the service, you discover there is data or repeated concerns that the software which the distance education patrons use to connect with the library is difficult to use and has the ability to negate or undermine the satisfaction with "customer experience" efforts on the part of library staff members. As the change leader, one needs to recognize this as a serious weakness that may not support the predefined performance standard. One will need to make some decisions about whether to continue the change initiative, but with realistically lowered expectations that the change will meet the desired performance standard, or one may need to recognize that there may be a different change initiative, using more stable and easier-to-use connection options, before embarking on the original change plan among the library staff.

When evaluating a change using the discrepancy evaluation model, it is important to look at the peripheral impact of the change through the four stages of organizational change: program definition, program installation, program process, and program product.[26] These represent the different aspects of a change initiative from the point of defining the change through the final resulting product. The last stage, program product, is often overlooked, as it is actually postimplementation. For example, suppose in implementing a change to fix a particular problem or offer a new service, has one created an entire new set of problems or caused confusion with another service, so that another change initiative must occur to address issues created by the original change initiative? This will show up if you are assessing the program product in the context of evaluating the discrepancy in how the change product conformed to the standard. Suppose you have led the implementation of a new book request model, but after the service is fully launched and implemented, you discover that patrons are badly confused between this request model that gets books for them from the main collection or through interlibrary loan and the purchase request service. You also discover that patrons expecting "their" library to purchase the book for them are not happy with an "access-focused" model that borrows the book from another library but may have more restrictions on how long an individual keeps the book. If this is the case, then one has to recognize that one was not entirely successful in several aspects of the original change initiative. Unfortunately, Provus's evaluation model focuses more on why there is a discrepancy rather than the discrepancy itself, but it lets one know that there is a gap in achieving success in the change initiative and serves as an indicator that further investigation is needed.

TYLER'S OBJECTIVE ATTAINMENT EVALUATION MODEL

The objective attainment model, commonly known as the goal-based evaluation model, is based on Ralph Tyler's 1949 evaluation model. This model is used to measure the actual performance of a new library service or change against its original identified objectives or goals to determine if the established goals were achieved.[27] Using both quantitative and qualitative methods, the change leader needs to design an evaluation to see how well the change achieved the goals and objectives of the new service and then begin collecting the needed data to compare to the stated objectives. This is the most commonly used evaluation model because unlike the goal-free model, this model allows the library administration to let the change manager know what the goals and objectives are. However, the problem with this type of model is that it doesn't take into consideration shifting goals and inconsistencies in goals.[28]

LEADERSHIP ASSESSMENT

Regardless of the evaluation models chosen and implemented, one aspect of assessing oneself as a change leader is to recognize when a change is not going successfully and step back from the commitment to the change before reaching the point of no return. Unfortunately, many leaders shy away from this because they think of deferring a change initiative that is not going well or reversing a decision that is not proving successful as a failure on their part, rather than exploring whether the change itself was just not appropriate at the time and under the current circumstances. Inconveniencing staff members by pushing them beyond their comfort zone or asking them to redesign workflows and processes as part of a change initiative is never a reason to defer or abandon a change. However, if one has pushed forward a change that leaves staff floundering under significantly increased workloads without the support of additional resources, then saying the change has been successful may reflect a tendency toward an isolationist or elitist perspective. One must have considered long-term sustainability as part of the planning part of the change. Unfortunately, changes that appear initially successful in the short term can be unsuccessful in the long term if staff support is not in place. As staff that went through the change decide to leave amidst a perception of being overworked and underappreciated, their replacements will be inheriting dysfunctional workflows. Additionally, from not having lived through the change, the new employees have a more superficial understanding, and supporting processes for the change will begin to falter.

There are numerous evaluation techniques that can be used to assess an individual's performance. The ones that work best in establishing how one has done as a change leader are those that gather input and data from all levels of the initiative in a full circle sort of approach. This would include information from the administrators that one reports upward to, often the basis of most annual appraisal models, as well as peer managers and the front-line employees and middle managers that actually implemented or were affected by the change. It is also important to seek specific information related to the explicit change initiative. Rather than asking the generic "How have I been doing?" or even "How have I been doing this year?" focus the questions on the change initiative. One can do this by asking, "Did I communicate effectively about when we needed to have particular milestones met?" or "Did I keep everyone informed of possible problems as they developed?" or "Did I handle the crisis from the delivery delay well?"

It is a characteristic of librarianship that we tend to be a "nice" profession where polite engagement is very important. Sometimes employees can mistake this niceness and courtesy for meaning one should not actually be critical of someone. When getting feedback on how one did, it may be that individuals are just not comfortable pointing out deficiencies to you directly, particularly if there is a long-term or personalized relationship. In this situation, it is important to bring in someone else to facilitate the gathering of comments. This usually should not be one's administrative supervisor because individuals will not want to say things that might "get you in trouble" or make them look bad within their hierarchy. Instead, one can look to a peer manager one is comfortable being open with, or even someone that was a grassroots leader from the change initiative with whom one has established a comfortable and open relationship.

However the detailed questions are asked, it is important to make sure that one has the data to answer the following questions:

How did I do as a leader for this change initiative?

What did I do well?

What did I do poorly?

What can I do to improve for next time?

When getting the feedback, it is important to receive it with an open mind. This means one should avoid marginalizing comments or feeling the need to defend oneself. If you find yourself saying, "Well, I knew they were not happy about that but there was nothing I could do about it" or "That feedback probably came from John, he was critical about everything," then you are already undermining the positives of the assessment process. If you did know of a problem and were not able to effectively address it, then you did not do it well and need to acknowledge that this is an area where one needs to develop skills and learn from the experience. The best compliment one can receive as a change leader is from staff members who admit to having been uncomfortable with or unsure about the change but who credit you with having helped them realize that the change was important, it was the right thing to do, and what was the best way to accomplish it while still taking pride in their job. This is the definition of successful contemporary change leadership.

KEYS TO SUCCESS

There is an extensive body of literature that can be referred to for more details on actual techniques for doing assessment in carrying out the concepts presented in this chapter. To be successful, one has to have an open attitude toward assessment.

- Try different informal and formal techniques to gather assessment data.
- Focus on discrete pieces of the process or change to avoid being overwhelmed by the evaluation process.
- Employ assessment activities throughout the entire change initiative, not just at the beginning to justify the change or at the end to create closure.
- Be open-minded in understanding and applying the information that comes back through the assessment process.
- Do not forget to seek evaluation of yourself as a change leader, and avoid the cycle of defensiveness or self-justification by responding in a positive model of continuous learning.

THINKING EXERCISES

1. Suppose you are leading an initiative that requires employees to cross-train into multiple service area tasks. What sort of assessment techniques might you do to evaluate the progress being made and identify possible barriers to the success of the change? (Hint: Since this involves individuals learning new tasks, assessments might include learning and critical thinking techniques from an educational or teaching perspective.)

2. As a result of a transaction model assessment survey during the implementation process, you discover that everyone is assuming that someone
else is responsible for a key part of changing an operational process.
What do you do to address this gap in coverage?

3. You have completed a change initiative that moved staff into a new work
area. You ask a peer manager to conduct a meeting to get feedback on
how you did in leading the change. You are not present at the meeting,
but your peer manager lets you know that several staff felt that you had
ignored or overridden their input about needing to leave space in the new
layout for supplies and book trucks to be stored. What do you do now? If
this is going to create ongoing workflow problems, is the change initiative really completed, or is this something you may still need to address
in some manner? What will you take away from this that you will use
when leading your next change initiative?

4. Think of the last change initiative you completed. Of the different types
of evaluation done at the end of the initiative, which would be the best fit
for assessing the result of the change? How well did the eventual change
correspond to the original intent or purpose of the change (goal-free
model, discretionary model, or objective attainment model)?

NOTES

1. Darlene Russ-Eft and Hallie Preskill, *Evaluation in Organizations: A Systematic Approach to Enhancing Learning, Performance, and Change* (Reading, MA: Perseus, 2001), 17.
2. Ron Alan Zimbalist, *The Human Factor in Change* (Lanham, MD: Scarecrow 2005), 125.
3. John Boulmetis and Phyllis Dutwin, *The ABC's of Evaluation: Timeless Techniques for Program and Project Managers,* 2nd ed. (San Francisco: Jossey-Bass, 2005), 4.
4. M. Scriven, *Evaluation Thesaurus*, 4th ed. (Thousand Oaks, CA: Sage, 1991), 340.
5. Jeannette Woodward, *Creating the Customer-Driven Academic Library* (Chicago: American Library Association, 2009).
6. Scriven, *Evaluation Thesaurus*, 340.
7. Russ-Eft and Preskill, *Evaluation in Organizations*.
8. P. H. Rossi and H. E. Freeman, *Evaluation: A Systematic Approach,* 3rd ed. (Thousand Oaks, CA: Sage, 1985).
9. M. C. Plantz, M. T. Greenway, and M. M. Hendricks, "Outcome Measurement: Showing Results in the Nonprofit Sector," *New Directions of Evaluation* 75 (1997): 15–30, 17.
10. M. Q. Patton. *Utilization-Focused Evaluations: The New Century Text* (Thousand Oaks, CA: Sage, 1997), 104.

11. M. Q. Patton, "Developmental Evaluation," *Evaluation Practice* 15, no. 3 (1994): 311–19, 313.
12. John M. Owen, *Program Evaluation: Forms and Approaches*, 3rd ed. (New York: Guilford, 2007).
13. Scriven, *Evaluation Thesaurus*.
14. S. B. Anderson and S. Ball, *The Profession and Practice of Program Evaluation* (San Francisco: Jossey-Bass, 1978), 3.
15. Boulmetis and Dutwin, *ABC's of Evaluation*.
16. Jay A. Conger, "The Dark Side of Leadership," in *Leading Organizations: Perspectives for a New Era*, ed. Gill Robinson Hickman (Thousand Oaks, CA: Sage, 1998), 250–60.
17. Boulmetis and Dutwin, *The ABC's of Evaluation*.
18. Ibid.
19. Ibid.
20. Conger, "The Dark Side of Leadership."
21. Russ-Eft and Preskill, *Evaluation in Organizations*.
22. Boulmetis and Dutwin, *The ABC's of Evaluation*.
23. Owen, *Program Evaluation*.
24. Conger, "The Dark Side of Leadership."
25. Andres Steinmetz, "The Discrepancy Evaluation Model," *Measurement in Education* 1, no. 7 (1976): 1–7.
26. Ibid.
27. Scriven, *Evaluation Thesaurus*, 178.
28. Boulmetis and Dutwin, *The ABC's of Evaluation*.

CHAPTER 9

CHANGE-SPECIFIC CHALLENGES

*They may forget what you said, but they will
never forget how you made them feel.*

—Carl W. Buechner

PREVIOUS CHAPTERS HAVE discussed change in a general sense, with particular
types of changes highlighted as examples in the context of leadership, communication,
planning, and engagement. While the overall framework in initiating, implementing,
and evaluating the success of a change stays the same, the actual details of the change
may require a particular communication style or troubleshooting technique. If you
think about it, you would use different approaches to launch and carry out a department organizational chart restructuring than you would to overhaul work spaces or
launch a new service. This chapter focuses more on different types of change initiatives and being aware of some of the specific issues that one has to anticipate and
address as a leader. However, some large-scale changes will involve multiple change
initiatives simultaneously, which can be overwhelming if they are not broken down
into manageable pieces. The chapter wraps up with some techniques for addressing
such a situational overload.

NEW ORGANIZATIONAL STRUCTURES

A unit restructuring or operational reorganization is a major change area that every
institution inevitably must address. Whether they are in response to external pressures such as competing Internet information services or internal pressures such as

employee turnover, through retirements or the departure of a key employee to take a position elsewhere, or to meet new service or operational initiatives, reorganizations are a function of every library.[1] Some library administrations see them as a change of last resort and try to keep overall units intact and with a similar structure, even as they have to change an individual librarian's primary assignment or role to meet an organizational need. These are the same libraries that will have a fairly transparent succession plan with a clearly identified heir apparent to leadership openings. Other library administrations see reorganizations as a preferred first option in addressing new initiatives, employee performance issues, or workflow concerns. Generally, once the implementation process begins, libraries with this second type of administration will see losses in staff jobs and the possibility of outsourcing these positions, such as original cataloging, library marketing, website development, and computer maintenance.[2] They view employees as flexible, fluid resources and reorganizations as individual and organizational growth opportunities. These organizations tend to restructure entire departments and change individual responsibilities on a regular, sometimes even annual, basis and often pride themselves on leading "lean and mean" libraries. Still others will occupy a middle ground of occasional staffing reorganizations of varying breadth.

How one will introduce and communicate about this change will differ depending on the organizational culture. If employees have limited experience or exposure to this type of change, their reactions may be driven more by fear or uncertainty, and reassurance is a key message to send. Similarly, employees may have developed deep personal connections in their unit structures, so the grieving elements will be more significant over perceived losses in relationships. For employees that have been through a lot of reorganizations, a change leader faces different challenges. In this situation, one will have to communicate with a focus on overcoming cynicism and a halfhearted buy-in toward the change by using words such as *adjustment* and *flexibility* to disguise the current situation in order to make employees think this reorganization will have positive outcomes for everyone. In reality, however, the library will once again be trying to press for greater efficiency from the same (or fewer) organizational resources.

The employees will be more likely to go along with the reorganization but not actually make a commitment to it because in the back of their minds they perceive it as a short-term issue that can be endured until the next change occurs. These staff will be less likely to have bonded as a team in a departmental structure and will have built relationships with peers based on nonwork commonality factors. As such, they will be less likely to see value to the reorganization. Adding to this problem as restructuring and downsizing continues (both inside and outside the organization), administrators become less likely to be proactive about employing behavioral management and communication strategies.[3]

Of the different types of organizational change, staffing reorganizations are the ones with the weakest foresight of how smoothly the implementation will actually proceed and what postchange fireworks will erupt. This is because in every aspect of this change, one is leading individual human beings who are all unique in their communication filters, skills, and personal and professional goals. Unfortunately, administrators and change leaders can easily slip into an authoritarian model when planning this type of change and delude themselves into thinking they have a complete understanding of individuals, know what is "best" for them and the organization, and how they will react. In truth, unless someone in a change leadership role has sat down with each person and in a truly open way had a discussion of the individual's goals and motivations, this is an erroneous assumption. Another mistake that some change leaders follow in planning a reorganization will be to open the discussion with a preliminary new organization chart with some names already penned in and then shut down discussion by calling these assignments "the obvious best fit." Once the change has begun in the implementation stage and even during the months following the reorganization, it will be important to keep individuals with mediation skill sets available to help with smoothing over disconnects. This will be particularly important during the formal evaluation cycle if there were supervisory changes. It may even be appropriate to add onto the change planning timeline a period of settling in and mediation and not declare the reorganization "finished" when the new finalized organizational charts are released, instead waiting until subsequent milestones are accomplished that testify to the organizational accomplishment that served as the prompt for the reorganization. As a result of the perceived continuing reorganizational change, the work atmosphere becomes a place employees must survive rather than where they work to advance themselves. This poor corporate climate becomes a place where staff loyalty and morale are low, and absenteeism is high. These feelings are increased where the employees feel trapped in their position because they believe that there are no longer opportunities for upward advancement.[4] Alternately, they can be frustrated at the feeling that they are administrative puppets, with no actual say in what their workplace role is to be.

SPACE CHANGES

Space changes cover a variety of situations that one may deal with in a library change initiative. The change could be a remodel of a public reading space, reconfiguring or shifting of the collection spaces, or changing employee work spaces. All three of these offer some common and unique challenges to the change leader. The challenges also vary widely based on the scope and breadth of the change. However, as Leighton and Weber stress when changing employees' work space, leaders must remember that "adequate accommodations for the library staff are essential for effective service."[5]

A typical commonality to all space changes is that one has only minimal control over the actual change. One will often be dealing with a number of third-party sub-contractors who will be working on their own schedules, from interior designers and furniture suppliers to construction/remodeling crews and inspectors. If the change involves external spaces, such as patios or green space, one's schedule will also be at the mercy of unpredictable weather. All of these factors are going to extend the time-line longer than one will want and introduce a number of frustrations. This will also introduce a greater need for effective crisis decision making as there are unexpected discoveries and details that arise that were not part of the original planning, such as electrical problems. It is important to avoid either inflating or deflating the role of the subcontractor and their impact. There is a tendency in libraries to be overly modest about our own skills and to value knowledge and expertise outside our own. However, as McDonald stresses, "Library managers must have a strong vision for the new library and this should inspire the designing and the whole building process."[6] In an effort to justify the expense, an administrator might give a professional interior designer, who has been brought in on a project, a big buildup and promise beautiful and functional spaces on the designer's behalf. Unfortunately, this establishes unrealistic expectations that do not allow for individual taste. Better to say the designer will bring in the current trends in colors and styles to make our spaces look less outdated or will recommend new furniture and fabrics that will endure the test of time and wear and that take into account the increasing use of computers.[7] Another aspect of using subcontractors comes when schedules start slipping. There is a natural tendency for those impacted by the unexpectedly extended period to look for rational causes and someone to blame. It will be important not to publicly vilify the subcontractor for problems that develop. To some degree, problems should be expected on any renovation project as there are generally unknowns, particularly in older buildings. Similarly, many subcontractors work with multiple clients simultaneously, and even though the project is your top priority, it will not be theirs. It is important to communicate and show acceptance and tolerance of this in laying out the planned change.

Another aspect of dealing with a space renovation is that one has to plan for alternate or interim space needs. These can be alternate work spaces for employees, staging space for the collection, or service desk relocations.[8] Thanks to the complete integration of technology into library workflows and services, it is no longer possible to shift the reference or circulation desk onto a card table with an extension cord. Instead, one must think about ergonomics and network cabling for the temporary space. This can also add to the stress of the change as staff members are asked to pack up and relocate multiple times or work in less-than-ideal, temporary conditions. In terms of a collection spatial move, this may mean having to double-handle books, with increased bending and lifting. Unless planned carefully, this can lead to an increase in injury claims. It will also be important to include as a follow-up a shelf-reading or inventory of the affected areas of the collection because no matter how careful everyone is, books will get mixed up in major shelving moves. In many ways, one is actually leading two changes, one away from the old space into a temporary, displaced, improvised environment and a second back to the renovated space.

One particular challenge when dealing with spatial-based changes is that some individuals can look at a drawing with schematics for chairs, tables, desks, and so on and extrapolate that to a three-dimensional perspective with ease and accuracy. However, others have difficulty translating a rectangle on a plan into a three-dimensional table in a space. These latter staff are likely to get into the new space and find that what they had previously approved does not actually work for them. This is why providing tools such as floor plans, furniture cutouts, floor planning software training, or even a "sample" desk configuration setup to help employees to redesign the space according to their workflow needs is so important and can be seen as an empowerment tool. According to Nixon, providing them with such tools also gets the group thinking about the space redesign in a required strategic direction.[9] Similarly, unless one has experienced working in a configuration, one may have difficulty recognizing if it will really work for them or not. One example of this is when people are configured with their backs to an open work area. They may not realize how uncomfortable they will be with people walking up behind them or just passing behind them until they have actually sat in the chair and felt the distraction.[10] Similarly, it can be difficult to predict noise from a drawing, particularly in open-office architecture environments. For these reasons, one must be patient as there are post-configuration discoveries that need adjustments.

One final note of leading a renovation or spatial change initiative is addressing staff curiosity and midchange realizations. In some cases, it may be necessary to set up pathways through the construction area to get from one area of the building to another, particularly where staff offices or student spaces have one main entrance. In other cases a space may be blocked off completely other than for a construction crew entrance and exit. Many people that choose to work in libraries have inquiring minds, and it can be difficult for them to not want to "sneak a peak" or look just a little closer. It will be important for you, as the project leader, to emphasize the importance of safety in setting rules of access. Similarly, those tantalizing glimpses can lead staff and patrons to jump to conclusions about the final look or configuration of the space. It will be important to continually keep stakeholders informed about the change but encourage them to hold their final opinions or concerns until they have seen the final results. Similarly, it will be important to constantly cast the décor in the context of the purpose of the space, clearly acknowledging that it may not be what everyone would want in their own living room or home office.

Sometimes, these glimpses or concerns can translate to comments back to subcontractors that can be interpreted as a change in instructions. This can be particularly problematic if the subcontractor already has questions about the plan. For example, suppose a work order or plan is unclear on which color a particular office wall is supposed to be painted. Or as the paint is going up, there is a realization that the visual flow does not lend itself to the color transition as well as everyone had thought. The worst-case scenario is where the contractor turns for clarification to someone working in the area who appears to be in charge, but in truth is not authorized to make the decision. As the change leader, one should establish clear lines for raising questions and issues of concern. Implicit in this is that one will take seriously and address concerns that are raised rather than ignore them, as the concerns may be quite legitimate and introduce safety issues. One should also be explicit in setting up the chain of command with the contractor on who has the authority to respond to questions or issue a hold order for further clarification.

PHILOSOPHICAL VISION CHANGES

One of the most difficult types of changes to carry forward is a change in the organizational philosophy or vision. The difficulty comes from the fact that verbal communication is the sole means of enacting the change. The philosophical change may drive subsequent changes in services, staffing, and space utilization. But without successful carry-through of the philosophical change, one is increasing the chance of long-term failure on these other change initiatives because the underlying philosophy supporting them has not been fully established in the organizational culture.[11] When attempting to lead a change of philosophy, it is critical to establish common base values as a foundation and be willing to work through differences of opinion in a way that reaches an accord. Trying to hierarchically force a change in values, particularly among professional librarians, will only undermine the success of the initiative. Instead, one must engage in a way that builds buy-in and engagement and allows room for debate and discussion.

A common mistake in leading this type of change is to want to rush through the philosophical change and quickly move on to the organizational service or spatial changes that provide a visible manifestation of the philosophical change. The reason this is a mistake is simply that if one has not evolved a culture that solidly supports the new philosophy, the other changes are undermined before they are started. Adding to this problem is if the organization's ethical beliefs and assumptions are entrenched in the organizational culture, then it will be even more difficult for the change leader to implement the change.[12] Additionally, in some institutions where librarians hold full faculty status, there may actually be rules or guidelines that must be followed as a part of a shared governance model. One ignores these rules at one's peril because not only will doing so hinder the success of future initiatives, it can also leave one open to allegations of noncompliance and jeopardize one's leadership position in the library.

In entering a philosophical change, one must be willing to discuss the new vision one has proposed, which means actually listening to concerns and responding to them in an explicit way. When dealing with a philosophical change, the change can actually come to resemble a religious conversion experience, where an administrator truly believes this change is necessary for the future survival of the organization. In this case, the leader begins "preaching" the message and assumes it is just a matter of saying the "right" words for others to see the light and join in. Unfortunately, this blind faith can block one from being an effective listener to the concerns being raised by others. It is important to maintain a level of skepticism, even as one is putting one's idea forward, and to not overlook legitimate concerns about local implementation of the philosophy.

THE BIG CHANGE

At the beginning of the chapter, it was mentioned that sometimes a change will be so massive that it will incorporate multiple changes in one initiative. If one is attempting to manage one of these massive initiatives, one must ground a philosophical change and establish buy-in before jumping into other changes that build on it. However, even when one has established the philosophical base, one may still be simultaneously addressing multiple reorganizations and space renovations at once. In this case, one needs to be aware of which staff may be influenced by which changes, either in a primary or secondary role, and where there is overlap. In doing so, it becomes important to recognize that some staff will be coming closer to the threshold of their ability to manage and incorporate the change. The reason for this, according to Hayes, is that it is not abnormal for some kinds of organizational change to upset and challenge the everyday work practices of management.[13]

For example, it might not seem that a reading room renovation on the second floor of building 1, recarpeting a public area on the first floor in building 2, remodeling a media room to include a podcasting facility on the third floor of building 1, and reallocating some shelving and public seating in the basement of building 2 would overlap that much. All of these areas are under different departments in the library. However, while one is blithely moving along with four different project leaders overseeing the four areas, one has burned out a facilities manager who has key coordination responsibilities for all of the projects. Similarly, in this same scenario, suppose the recarpeting project blocks access to a freight elevator that the basement change group was counting on using to move shelving in. Inevitably tempers flare and problems erupt. In these cases, collaboration and having someone with authority to speak out in a central oversight position are essential.

Complex change projects can also significantly reduce the change resilience of individuals and simply wear them out. Suppose in order to do a particular major renovation, staff are required to relocate three different times because of the staged phases of the construction. It is important to realize that each relocation is more than just packing a few files in a box. In actuality our workflows are largely driven by habit, and having to consciously change habits can be a big undertaking. It might not sound like it is such a big deal for staff members who were in a desk arrangement with drawers on the right and an open space for a book truck on the left to be moved into another desk that has the open space for the book truck on the right and desk drawers on the left. In truth, it will be a difficult adjustment for them to break the habit of reaching in a particular direction. In a sense, one is redefining all of one's workflow behaviors. Then just about the time one has trained to the new habits of reaching to the left for files and right for the books, one has to change again back in the new space and start all over again. If at the same time individuals are trying to build a positive relationship with new supervisors by impressing them and instead feel like they are appearing to be klutzy or disorganized, then the individuals' stress level will go up and overall confidence will go down. It is important to realize what depths of subliminal behavior are actually be affected by changes and to encourage patience and acceptance when these changes are multistaged or intersecting.

There is one final point to examine when talking about highly complex changes. Because of realistic limitations, such as having one or two particularly strong mid-level change leaders or, from the example earlier, a single facilities coordinator who can only monitor so many simultaneous construction projects at once, some leaders of large change initiatives will decide to break them out into smaller pieces. However, Whittington's large-scale survey of organizational change indicates positive returns when system-wide rather than piecemeal change was introduced into an organization.[14] This positive return can be related to Vakola and Nikolaou's findings that there was a negative parallel between job stress, caused by organizational change, and employees' feelings toward this change. Vakola and Nikolaou discovered that employees who were stressed showed a decrease in organizational commitment and an unwillingness to accept organizational change interventions.[15] Consequently, ongoing continuous small or midlevel changes are actually harder on staff from an emotional perspective than having their entire workplace world put through an upheaval.[16] This is because with the continuous change, there is never the opportunity to actually get one's feet under one and establish a foundation one can build on professionally. Instead, like being in the ocean, one is pushed over time and again as each wave comes rolling in. For this reason, it is important for leaders of major change initiatives to realize the importance of laying out the entire large-change picture at the start, rather than get through one change, only to announce another the next day.

KEYS TO SUCCESS

In being an effective change leader, it is important to realize that not all changes are the same and one should

- gather information on how different changes impact an individual
- consider how much individuals are being asked to change and what the scope of the change really means for them
- modify one's expectations when changes are overlapping and intersecting
- continually revisit whether one has missed communicating with secondary and tertiary stakeholders
- accept that the employees are not an easily renewable resource and that one's consideration of their needs and emotions will better position one for long-term success in leading future changes.

THINKING EXERCISES

1. You are leading a change to merge two separate departments (such as acquisitions and cataloging or interlibrary services and circulation). What particular challenges will you face in the interpersonal relationships between these departments?

2. The staff in a unit that had previously occupied individual offices are being relocated to a new workspace that is configured in an open-floor-plan, cubicle model with 4-foot temporary partitions separating them. What are some of the challenges you will face in leading this change? (Hint: What are employees giving up?) What can you do to offer opportunities to engage in the change for the individual staff members?

3. The dean has asked you to identify services that can be modified for more user-driven self-sufficiency (such as requesting a book be purchased, offering self checkout, etc.). Your staff are having trouble accepting this new direction where they do not mediate transactions as directly. How would you explain and encourage support of this vision/philosophy to them?

4. As a part of the unit merger referenced in exercise 1, the staff will also be relocated and integrated into a new space and are charged to rethink workflows for more efficiency. How are you going to tackle such a massive change? What are some milestones you will use to track the progress of the change?

NOTES

1. Paul M. Hirsch and Michaela De Soucey, "Organizational Restructuring and Its Consequences: Rhetorical and Structural," *Annual Review of Sociology* 32 (2006): 171–89.
2. Ibid.
3. Doris A. Van Horn-Christopher, "Perceived Communication Barriers between Management and Support Staff Personnel Undergoing Organizational Restructuring," *American Business Review,* June 1996, 95–107.
4. Ibid.
5. Philip D. Leighton and David C. Weber, *Planning Academic and Research Library Buildings,* 3rd ed. (Chicago: American Library Association, 1999), 289.
6. Andrew McDonald, "The Ten Commandments Revisited: The Qualities of Good Library Space," *Liber Quarterly: Journal of European Research Libraries* 16, no. 2 (2006): 13–29.

7. Virginia J. Kelsh, "Build It Right and They Will Come: The Librarian's Role in Library Construction," *Law Library Journal* 98, no. 2 (2006): 269–86.

8. Gail L. Persily and Karen A. Butter, "Reinvisioning and Redesigning 'A Library for the Fifteenth through Twenty-First Centuries': A Case Study on Loss of Space from the Library and Center for Knowledge Management, University of California, San Francisco," *Journal of Medical Library Association* 98, no. 1 (January 2010): 44–48.

9. Judith M. Nixon, "A Library Staff Becomes a Team," *Journal of Business and Finance Librarianship* 4, no. 4 (1999): 31–47.

10. Wyoma vanDuinkerken and Pixey Anne Mosley, "Increasing Investment through Participation: Redoing Workspace Layouts without Tears and Angst," *Library Leadership and Management* 23, no. 1 (2009): 5–11.

11. Donald L. Anderson, *Organization Development: The Process of Leading Organizational Change* (Thousand Oaks, CA: Sage, 2010), 26–27.

12. Ibid., 263

13. John Hayes, *The Theory and Practice of Change Management* (New York: Palgrave, 2002), 166.

14. Richard Whittington and others, "Change and Complementarities in the New Competitive Landscape: A European Panel Study 1992–1996," *Organizational Science* 10, no. 5 (1999): 583–600, 597.

15. Maria Vakola and Ioannis Nikolaou, "Attitudes Towards Organizational Change: What Is the Role of Employees' Stress and Commitment?" *Employee Relations* 27, no. 2: 160–74.

16. Whittington, "Change and Complementarities."

WORKS CITED

Adeyoyin, Samuel Olu. "Managing the Library's Corporate Culture for Organizational Efficiency, Productivity, and Enhanced Service." *Library Philosophy and Practice* 3 (Spring 2006): 1–14.

Agrawal, Anup, Charles R. Knoeber, and Theofanis Tsoulouhas. "Are Outsiders Handicapped in CEO Successions?" *Journal of Corporate Finance* 12 (2006): 619–44.

Albright, L., D. A. Kenny, and T. E. Malloy. "Consensus in Personality Judgments at Zero Acquaintance." *Journal of Personality and Social Psychology* 55 (1988): 387–95.

Ambady, N., and R. Rosenthal. "Thin Slices of Expressive Behavior as Predictors of Interpersonal Consequences: A Meta-Analysis." *Psychological Bulletin* 11 (1992): 256–74.

American Library Association. "Second Congress on Professional Education, November 17–19, 2000, Final Report of the Steering Committee." www.ala.org/ala/education careers/education/2ndcongressonpro/2ndcongressprofessionaleducationfinal.cfm.

Anderson, Donald L. *Organization Development: The Process of Leading Organizational Change.* Thousand Oaks, CA: Sage, 2010 .

Anderson, S. B., and S. Ball. *The Profession and Practice of Program Evaluation.* San Francisco: Jossey-Bass, 1978.

Anderson-Cook, Christine M. "More Damned Lies and Statistics: How Numbers Confuse Public Issues/Change: A Guide to Gambling, Love, the Stock Market, & Just About Everything Else." *American Statistician* 59, no. 3 (2005): 274–75.

Arouet, François-Marie. *Dictionnaire Philosophique Portatif.* London, 1765.

Armstrong, Michael. *A Handbook of Personnel Management Practice.* 4th edition. London: Kogan Page, 1991.

Bakker, Arnold, and Wilmar Schaufeli. "Positive Organizational Behavior: Engaged Employees in Flourishing Organizitions," *Journal of Organizational Behavior* 29, no. 2 (2008): 147–54.

Bartunek, Jean M., and others. "Managers and Project Leaders: Conducting Their Own Action Research Interventions." In *Handbook of Organizational Consultation*, edited by Robert T. Golembiewski. 2nd edition. New York: Marcel Dekker, 2000.

Battin, Patricia. "Leadership in a Transformational Age." In *Mirage of Continuity: Reconfiguring Academic Information Resources for the 21st Century*, edited by Brian L. Hawkins and Patricia Battin. Washington, DC: Council on Library and Information Resources, Association of American Universities, 1998: 271–77.

Beck, Aaron T. "Beyond Belief: A Theory of Modes, Personality, and Psychopathology." In *Frontiers of Cognitive Therapy*, edited by Paul M. Salkovskis. New York: Guilford, 1996.

Bennis, Warren. *Managing People Is Like Herding Cats.* Provo, UT: Executive Excellence, 1997.

Beugelsdijk, Sjoerd, Carla Koen, and Niels Noorderhaven. "A Dyadic Approach to the Impact of Differences in Organizational Culture on Relationship Performance." *Industrial Marketing Management* 38 (2009): 312–23.

Boulmetis, John, and Phyllis Dutwin. *The ABC's of Evaluation: Timeless Techniques for Program and Project Managers.* 2nd edition. San Francisco: Jossey-Bass, 2005.

Bridges, William. *Managing Transitions: Making the Most of Change.* 2nd edition. Cambridge, MA: Perseus, 2003.

Brown, Martha A. "Values—A Necessary but Neglected Ingredient of Motivation on the Job." *Academy of Management Review* 1 (October 1976): 12–23.

Brunstein, Joachim C. "Motivation and Performance Following Failure: The Effortful Pursuit of Self-Defining Goals." *Applied Psychology: An International Review* 49, no. 1 (2000): 340–56.

Carnall, Colin. *The Change Management Toolkit.* London: Thomson, 2003.

Cawsey, Tupper, and Gene Deszca. *Toolkit for Organizational Change.* Los Angeles: Sage, 2007.

Cervone, H. Frank. "Working through Resistance to Change by Using the Competing Commitments Model." *International Digital Library Perspectives* 23, no. 3 (2007): 250–53.

Confederation of British Industry. *The Lost Billions: Annual Healthcare Survey of Absence and Turnover 2002.* London: Confederation of British Industry/AXA PPP Healthcare, 2003.

Conger, Jay A. "The Dark Side of Leadership." In *Leading Organizations: Perspectives for a New Era*, edited by Gill Robinson Hickman. Thousand Oaks, CA: Sage, 1998.

Cooney, Richard, and Graham Sewell. "Shaping the Other: Maintaining Expert Managerial Status in a Complex Change Management Program." *Group and Organization Management* 33 (December 2008): 685–711.

Cronin, Blaise. "Knowledge Management, Organizational Culture and Anglo-American Higher Education." *Journal of Information Science* 27, no. 3 (2001): 129–37.

Curzon, Susan Carol. *Managing Change: A How-to-Do-It Manual for Librarians.* Revised edition. London: Facet, 2006.

Deal, Terrence E., and Allan A. Kennedy. *Corporate Cultures: The Rites and Rituals of Corporate Life.* Reading, MA: Addison-Wesley, 1982.

Deming, William Edwards. *Out of the Crisis.* Cambridge, MA: MIT Press, 1986.

Dent, Eric B., and Susan Galloway Goldberg. "Challenging 'Resistance to Change.'" *Journal of Applied Behavioral Science* 35 (March 1999): 25–41.

DesRoches, Brian. *Your Boss Is Not Your Mother: Breaking Free from Emotional Politics to Achieve Independence and Success at Work.* New York: Morrow, 1995.

Dose, Jennifer. "Work Values: An Integrative Framework and Illustrative Application to Organizational Socialization." *Journal of Occupational and Organizational Psychology* 70 (1997): 219–40.

Downey, Diane. "HR's Role in Assimilating New Leaders." *Employment Relations Today,* Winter 2002: 69–83.

Elsaid, Eahab, and Wallace N. Davison. "What Happened to CEO Compensation Following Turnover and Succession?" *Quarterly Review of Economics and Finance* 49, no. 2 (2009): 424–47.

Erturk, Alper. "A Trust-Based Approach to Promote Employees' Openness to Organizational Change in Turkey." *International Journal of Manpower* 29, no. 5 (2008): 462–83.

Feigenbaum, Armand V. *Quality Control: Principles, Practice, and Administration.* McGraw-Hill, Collins, 2001.

Fernandez, Sergio, and Hal G. Rainey. "Managing Successful Organizational Change in the Public Sector." *Public Administration Review* (March/April 2006): 168–76.

Ferris, Stephen P., Zuobao Wei, and Shaorong Zhang. "CEO Succession, Incentives and Firm Performance: Insiders versus Outsiders." http://69.175.2.130/~finman/Orlando/Papers/CEO_FWZ_07.pdf.

Foegen, Joseph H. "Why Not Empowerment?" *Business and Economic Review* 45 (April–June 1999): 31–33.

Folinas, Dimitris, and others. "E-volution of a Supply Chain: Cases and Best Practices." *Internet Research* 14, no. 4 (2004): 274–83.

Fronda, Yannick, and Jean-Luc Moriceau. "I Am Not Your Hero: Change Management and Culture Shocks in a Public Sector Corporation." *Journal of Organizational Change Management* 21, no. 5 (2008): 589–609.

Gagné, Marylène, and Edward L. Deci. "Self-Determination Theory and Work Motivation." *Journal of Organizational Behavior* 26 (2005): 331–62.

Gallagher, Carolyn, and others. "Implementing Organizational Change." In *Implementing Organizational Interventions: Steps, Processes, and Best Practices,* edited by Jerry W. Hedge and Elaine D. Pulakos. San Francisco: Jossey-Bass, 2002.

Gotsill, Gina, and Meryl Natchez. "From Resistance to Acceptance: How to Implement Change Management." *T+D,* November 2007.

Grant, Anthony M. "Workplace and Executive Coaching: A Bibliography from the Scholarly Business Literature." In *Evidence-Based Coaching Handbook: Putting Best Practices to Work for Your Clients,* edited by Dianne R. Stober and Anthony M. Grant. Hoboken, NJ: Wiley, 2006.

Green, Mike. *Change Management Masterclass: A Step by Step Guide to Successful Change.* Philadelphia: Kogan Page, 2007.

Haevey, Thomas R. *Checklist for Change: A Pragmatic Approach to Creating and Controlling Change.* 2nd edition. Lancaster, PA: Technomic, 1995.

Haidt, Jonathan. "The Emotional Dog and Its Rational Tail: A Social Intuitionist Approach to Moral Judgment." *Psychological Review* 108, no. 4 (2001): 814–34.

Hall, G., and S. Hord. "Stages of Concern Questionnaire." In *Implementing Change: Patterns, Principles, and Potholes.* Boston: Allyn and Bacon, 2006.

Hammer, Michael, and Steven Stanton. *The Reengineering Revolution: A Handbook.* New York: HarperBusiness, 1995.

Handy, Charles B. *Understanding Organisations.* Harmondsworth, UK: Penguin Books, 1985.

Harrison, D. Brian, and Maurice D. Pratt. "A Methodology for Reengineering Businesses." *Strategic Leadership* 21, no. 2 (1993): 6–11.

Hayes, John. *The Theory and Practice of Change Management.* 3rd edition. Basingstoke, NY: Palgrave Macmillan, 2010.

Hedge, Jerry W., and Elaine D. Pulakos. "Grappling with Implementation: Some Preliminary Thoughts and Relevant Research." In *Implementing Organizational Interventions: Steps, Processes, and Best Practices,* edited by Jerry W. Hedge and Elaine D. Pulakos. San Francisco: Jossey-Bass, 2002.

Heinz, Lisa C. "White Lies, Damned Lies and Statistics." *Engineering and Science* (Fall 1989): 19–23.

Hirsch, Paul M., and Michaela De Soucey. "Organizational Restructuring and Its Consequences: Rhetorical and Structural." *Annual Review of Sociology* 32 (2006): 171–89.

Hise, P. "Chart Showing Amounts of Time CEOs Spend on Various Human-Resources Issues." *Motivation Inclination Inc.* 15, no. 8 (1993): 28.

Holtz, Shel. *Corporate Conversations: A Guide to Crafting Effective and Appropriate Internal Communications.* New York: Amacom, 2004.

Jordan, Ann T. *Business Anthropology* (Prospect Heights, IL: Waveland, 2003), 85.

Jurkiewicz, Carole L., Tom K. Massey, and Roger G. Brown. "Motivation in Public and Private Organizations: A Comparative Study." *Public Productivity and Management Review* 21, no. 3 (1998): 230–50.

Kanter, Rosabeth Moss, and Barry Stein. *The Challenge of Organizational Change: How Companies Experience It and Leaders Guide It.* New York: Free Press, 1992.

Kegan, Robert, and Lisa Laskow Lehey. "The Real Reason People Won't Change." *Harvard Business Review* (November 2001): 85–92.

Kelsh, Virginia J. "Build It Right and They Will Come: The Librarian's Role in Library Construction." *Law Library Journal* 98, no. 2 (2006): 269–86.

Kitchen, Philip J., and Finbarr Daly. "Internal Communication during Change Management." *Corporate Communications* 7, no. 1 (2002): 46–53.

Kotter, John P. "Leading Change: Why Transformation Efforts Fail." *Harvard Business Review* 73, no. 2 (1995): 59–67.

Kotter, John P., and Leonard A. Schlesinger. "Choosing Strategies for Change." *Harvard Business Review* (March-April 1979): 106–14.

Kreitz, Patricia A. "Best Practices for Managing Organizational Diversity." *Journal of Academic Librarianship* 34 (March 2008): 101–20.

Kubler-Ross, Elisabeth. *On Death and Dying.* New York: Macmillan, 1969.

Lakos, Amos, and Shelley Phipps. "Creating a Culture of Assessment: A Catalyst for Organizational Change." *Portal: Libraries and the Academy* 4, no. 3 (2004): 345–61.

Laszlo, Christopher, and Jean-François Laugel. *Large-Scale Organizational Change: An Executive's Guide.* Woburn, MA: Butterworth-Heinemann, 2000.

Leban, Bill, and Romuald Stone. *Managing Organizational Change*. 2nd edition. New Jersey: John Wiley, 2008.

Leighton, Philip D., and David C. Weber. *Planning Academic and Research Library Buildings*. 3rd edition. Chicago: American Library Association, 1999.

Lewin, Kurt. "Action Research and Minority Problems." *Journal of Social Issues* 2 (1946): 34–46.

Lewis, Gerald. *Organizational Crisis Management: The Human Factor*. New York: Auerbach, 2006.

Lewis, Laurie K., and others. "Advice on Communicating during Organizational Change." *Journal of Business Communication* 43, no. 2 (2006): 113–37.

Lippitt, Gordon L., and others. *Implementing Organizational Change: A Practical Guide to Managing Change Efforts*. San Francisco: Jossey-Bass, 1985.

Little, Beverly, and Philip Little. "Employee Engagement: Conceptual Issues." *Journal of Organizational Culture, Communications and Conflict* 10, no. 1 (2006): 111–20.

Lohela, Malin, and others. "Does a Change in Psychosocial Work Factors Lead to a Change in Employee Health?" *Journal of Occupational and Environmental Medicine* 51, no. 2 (2009): 195–203.

Lucus, Leyland M. "The Impact of Trust and Reputation on the Transfer of Best Practices." *Journal of Knowledge Management* 9, no. 4 (2005): 87–101.

Lussier, Robert N., and Christopher F. Achua. *Leadership: Theory, Application, Skill Development*. 4th edition. Mason, OH: Thomson/South-Wester, 2009.

Majanovic, Olivera. "Supporting the 'Soft' Side of Business Process Reengineering." *Business Process Management Journal* 6, no. 1 (2000): 43–55.

Martin, M. Jason. "That's the Way We Do Things Around Here: An Overview of Organizational Culture." *Electronic Journal of Academic and Special Librarianship* 7 (Spring 2006), http://southernlibrarianship.icaap.org/content/v07n01/martin_m01.htm (accessed September 16, 2010).

Mayo Clinic staff. "Seasonal Affective Disorder (SAD)." 2009. www.mayoclinic.com/health/seasonal-affective-disorder/ds00195.

McDonald, Andrew. "The Ten Commandments Revisited: The Qualities of Good Library Space." *Liber Quarterly: Journal of European Research Libraries* 16, no. 2 (2006): 13–29.

Meglino, Bruce, Elizabeth Ravlin, and Cheryl Adkins. "Value Congruence and Satisfaction with a Leader: An Examination of the Role of Interaction." *Human Relations* 44 (May 1991): 481–95.

Miller, Danny. "Stale in the Saddle: CEO Tenure and the Match between Organization and Environment." *Management Science* 37, no. 1 (1991): 34–52.

Miller, Danny, and Jamal Shamsie. "Learning across the Life Cycle: Experimentation and Performance among Hollywood Studio Heads." *Strategic Management Journal* 22, no. 8 (2001): 725–45.

Mohan, Kannan, Peng Xu, and Balasubramaniam Ramesh. "Improving the Change-Management Process." *Communication of the ACM* 51 (May 2008): 59–64.

Montgomery, Carol Hansen, and JoAnne L. Sparks. "The Transition to an Electronic Journal Collection: Managing the Organizational Changes." *Serials Review* 26, no. 3 (2000): 4–18.

Montgomery, Jack G., and Eleanor I. Cook. *Conflict Management for Libraries: Strategies for a Positive, Productive Workplace*. Chicago: American Library Association, 2005.

Morgan, Gareth. *Images of Organization.* Beverly Hills, CA: Sage, 1986.

Morrell, Kevin M., and others. "Organizational Change and Employee Turnover." *Personnel Review* 33, no. 2 (2004): 161–73.

Morrison, Elizabeth Wolfe, and Frances J. Milliken. "Organizational Silence: A Barrier to Change and Development in a Pluralistic World." *Academy of Management Review* 25 (October 2000): 706–25.

Mosley, Pixey Anne. "Mentoring Gen X Managers: Tomorrow's Library Leadership Is Already Here." *Library Administration & Management* 19, no. 4 (Fall 2005): 185–92.

Munde, Gail. "Beyond Mentoring: Toward the Rejuvenation of Academic Libraries." *Journal of Academic Librarianship* 26 (May 2000): 171–75.

Murphy, Lawrence, and Steven Sauter. "The USA Perspective: Current Issues and Trends in the Management of Work Stress." *Australian Psychologist* 38 (July 2003): 151–57.

Nelson, Sandra. *Strategic Planning for Results.* Chicago: American Library Association, 2008.

———. *Implementing for Results.* Chicago: American Library Association, 2009.

Nemeth, C. J. "Managing Innovation: When Less Is More." *California Management Review* 40, no. 1 (1997): 59–74.

Nicely, Donna, and Beth Dempsey. "Building a Culture of Leadership: ULC's Executive Leadership Institute Fills Libraries' Biggest Training Void." *Public Libraries* 44 (2005): 297–300.

Nicholson, N. "The Transition Cycle: Causes, Outcomes, Processes, and Forms." In *On the Move: The Psychology of Change and Transition,* edited by S. Fisher and C. L. Cooper. London: John Wiley and Sons, 1990.

Nilakant, V., and S. Ramnarayan. *Change Management: Altering Mindset in a Global Context.* California: Sage, 2006.

Nixon, Judith M. "A Library Staff Becomes a Team." *Journal of Business and Finance Librarianship* 4, no. 4 (1999): 31–47.

Nodfor, Hermann Achidi, and others. "What Does the New Boss Think? How New Leaders' Cognitive Communities and Recent 'Top Down' Success Affect Organizational Change and Performance." *Leadership Quarterly* 20 (2009): 799–813.

Oreg, Shaul. "Personality, Context, and Resistance to Organizational Change." *European Journal of Work and Organizational Psychology* 15, no. 1 (2006): 73–101.

Owen, John M. Program *Evaluation: Forms and Approaches.* 3rd edition. New York: Guilford, 2007.

Paraskevas, Alexandros. "Crisis Management or Crisis Response System: A Complexity Science Approach to Organizational Crisis." *Management Decision* 44, no. 7 (2006): 892–907.

Pardo del Val, Manuela, and Clara Martinez Fuentes. "Resistance to Change: A Literature Review and Empirical Study." *Journal of Management Decision* 41, no. 2 (2003): 148–55.

Paton, Robert A. and James McCalman. *Change Management: A Guide to Effective Implementation.* 3rd edition. Los Angeles: Sage, 2008.

Patton, M. Q. *Utilization-Focused Evaluations: The New Century Text.* Thousand Oaks, CA: Sage, 1997.

Patton, M. Q. "Developmental Evaluation." *Evaluation Practice* 15, no. 3 (1994): 311–19, 313.

Perrow, Charles. *Normal Accidents: Living with High-Risk Technologies.* Princeton, NJ: Princeton University Press, 1999.

Persily, Gail L., and Karen A. Butter. "Reinvisioning and Redesigning 'A Library for the Fifteenth through Twenty-First Centuries': A Case Study on Loss of Space from the Library and Center for Knowledge Management, University of California, San Francisco." *Journal of Medical Library Association* 98, no. 1 (January 2010): 44–48.

Peters, Thomas, and Robert Waterman. *In Search of Excellence: Lessons from America's Best-Run Companies.* New York: Harper & Row, 1982.

Pfeffer, Jeffrey. *Competitive Advantage through People.* Boston: Harvard Business School Press, 1994.

Piderit, Sandy Kristin. "Rethinking Resistance and Recognizing Ambivalence: A Multidimensional View of Attitudes Toward an Organizational Change." *Academy of Management* 25, no. 4 (2000): 783–94.

Plantz, M. C., M. T. Greenway, and M. M. Hendricks. "Outcome Measurement: Showing Results in the Nonprofit Sector." *New Directions of Evaluation* 75 (1997): 15–30, 17.

Porac, Joseph F., Howard Thomas, and Charles Baden-Fuller. "Competitive Groups as Cognitive Communities: The Case of Scottish Knitwear Manufacturers." *Journal of Management Studies* 26, no. 4 (2007): 397–416.

Powell, General (Ret.) Colin. 2nd Brigade Combat Team of the 28th Infantry Division, *Iron Soldier Newsletter,* February 15, 2006.

Rabin, Matthew, and Joel L. Schrag. "First Impressions Matter: A Model of Confirmatory Bias." *Quarterly Journal of Economics* 114, no. 1 (1999): 37–82.

Rafferty, Alannah E., and Mark A. Griffin. "Perceptions of Organizational Change: A Stress and Coping Perspective." *Journal of Applied Psychology* 91, no. 5 (2006): 1154–62.

Rieple, Alison. "The Paradoxes of New Managers as Levers of Organizational Change." *Strategic Change* 7 (1997): 211–25.

Riggs, Donald E. "What's in Store for Academic Libraries? Leadership and Management Issues." *Journal of Academic Librarianship* 23 (January 1997): 3–7.

Roger, Derek. "Psychometrics: Lies, Damn Lies, and Statistics?" *Human Resources Magazine* 14, no. 2 (2009): 16–17.

Rossi, P. H., and H. E. Freeman. *Evaluation: A Systematic Approach.* 3rd edition. Thousand Oaks, CA: Sage, 1985.

Ruff, Peter, and Khalid Aziz. *Managing Communications in a Crisis.* Burlington, VT: Gower, 2003.

Russ-Eft, Darlene, and Hallie Preskill. *Evaluation in Organizations: A Systematic Approach to Enhancing Learning, Performance, and Change.* Reading, MA: Perseus, 2001.

Ryan, Kathleen D., and Daniel K. Oestreich. *Driving Fear Out of the Workplace: How to Overcome the Invisible Barriers to Quality, Productivity and Innovation.* San Francisco: Jossey-Bass, 1991.

Rynes, Sara L., Barry Gerhart, and Kathleen A. Minette. "The Importance of Pay in Employee Motivation: Discrepancies Between What People Say and What They Do." *Human Resource Management* 43, no. 4 (2004): 381.

Saksvik, Per Oystein, and others. "Developing Criteria for Healthy Organizational Change." *Work and Stress* 21 (July-September, 2007): 243–63.

Saunders, David M., and others. "Employee Voice to Supervisors." Employee *Responsibilities and Rights Journal* 5 (September 1992): 241–59.

Schein, Edgar. "Organizational Culture and Leadership." In *Classics of Organization Theory,* edited by Jay Shafritz and J. Steven Ott. Fort Worth: Harcourt College, 2001, 373–74.

———. *Organizational Culture and Leadership.* San Francisco: Jossey-Bass 1985.

Scriven, M. *Evaluation Thesaurus.* 4th edition. Thousand Oaks, CA: Sage, 1991.

Seeger, Matthew Wayne, and others. *Communication and Organizational Crisis.* Westport, CT: Greenwood, 2003.

Seijts, Gerard H., and Dan Crim. "What Engages Employees the Most, or, The Ten C's of Employee Engagement." *Ivery Business Journal* (March/April 2006): 1–5.

Shaw, Wade H. "Celebrating the Leadership of Peter F. Drucker." *IEEE Engineering Management Review* 34, no. 2 (2006): 2.

Shen, Wei, and Albert A. Cannella Jr. "Revisiting the Performance Consequences of CEO Succession: The Impacts of Succession Type, Post-Succession Senior Executive Turnover, and Departing CEO Tenure." *Academy of Management Journal* 45, no. 4 (2002): 717–33.

Smeltzer, Larry R. "An Analysis of Strategies for Announcing Organizational-Wide Change." *Group and Organizational Studies* 16, no. 1 (1991): 5–24.

Smith, Ian. "Continuing Professional Development and Workplace Learning: Achieving Successful Organizational Change—Do's and Don'ts of Change Management." *Library Management* 27, no. 4/5 (2006): 300–306.

Smith, Peter B., and Mark F. Peterson. *Leadership, Organizations and Culture.* London: Sage, 1988.

Spector, Bert. *Implementing Organizational Change: Theory and Practice.* New Jersey: Prentice Hall, 2007.

Spreitzer, Gretchen. "Psychological Empowerment in the Workplace: Dimensions, Measurement, and Validation." *Academy of Management Journal* 38, no. 5 (1995): 1442–65.

Steinmetz, Andres. "The Discrepancy Evaluation Model." *Measurement in Education* 1, no. 7 (1976): 1–7.

Stephens, Denise, and Keith Russell. "Organizational Development, Leadership, Change, and the Future of Libraries." *Library Trend* 53 (Summer 2004): 238–57.

Stober, Dianne R. "Making It Stick: Coaching as a Tool for Organizational Change." *Coaching: An International Journal of Theory, Research and Practice* 1, no. 1 (2008): 71–80.

Strebel, Paul. "Why Do Employees Resist Change?" *Harvard Business Review* 74 (May–June 1996): 86–92.

Swanson, Vivien, and Kevin Power. "Employees' Perceptions of Organizational Restructuring: The Role of Social Support." *Work & Stress* 15, no. 2 (2001): 161–78.

Tannen, Deborah. "Women and Men in Conversations." In *The Workings of Language: From Prescriptions to Perspectives,* edited by Rebecca S. Wheeler. Westport, CT: Praeger, 1999.

Tvedt, Sturle D., Per Oystein Saksvik, and Kjell Nytro. "Does Change Process Healthiness Reduce the Negative Effects of Organizational Change on the

Psychosocial Work Environment?" *Work and Stress* 23 (January-March 2009): 80–98.

Vakola, Maria, and Ioannis Nikolaou. "Attitudes Towards Organizational Change: What Is the Role of Employees' Stress and Commitment?" *Employee Relations* 27, no. 2: 160–74.

Van Horn-Christopher, Doris A. "Perceived Communication Barriers between Management and Support Staff Personnel Undergoing Organizational Restructuring." *American Business Review,* June 1996, 95–107.

vanDuinkerken, Wyoma, and Pixey Anne Mosley. "Increasing Investment through Participation: Redoing Workspace Layouts without Tears and Angst." *Library Leadership and Management* 23, no. 1 (2009): 5–11.

Von Dran, Gisela M., and Jennifer Cargill, editors. *Catalysts for Change.* New York: Haworth, 1993.

Warnken, Paula. "The Impact of Technology on Information Literacy Education in Libraries." *Journal of Academic Librarianship* 30 (March 2004): 151–56.

Whittington, Richard, and others. "Change and Complementarities in the New Competitive Landscape: A European Panel Study 1992–1996." *Organizational Science* 10, no. 5 (1999): 583–600, 597.

Wiegand, Wayne A., and Donald G. Davis. *Encyclopedia of Library History.* New York: Garland, 1994.

Williamson, Vicki. "Relationships and Engagement: The Challenges and Opportunities for Effective Leadership and Change Management in a Canadian Research Library." *Library Management* 29, nos. 1/2 (2008): 29–40.

Woodruff, Davis M. "How to Effectively Manage Change." *Hydrocarbon Processing* 75, no. 1 (1996): 145.

Woodward, Jeannette. *Creating the Customer-Driven Academic Library.* Chicago: American Library Association, 2009.

Woodward, Sally, and Chris Hendry. "Leading and Coping with Change." *Journal of Change Management* 4 (June 2004): 155–83.

Yu, Ming-Chu. "Employees' Perception of Organizational Change: The Mediating Effects of Stress Management Strategies." *Public Personnel Management* 38, no. 1 (2009): 17–32.

Zimbalist, Ron Alan. *The Human Factor in Change.* Lanham, MD: Scarecrow 2005.

INDEX

You may also be interested in

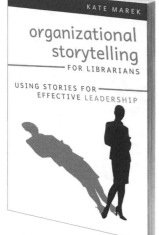